Visitor's Guide to Bermuda
3rd Edition

By Blair Howard

Table of Contents

Introduction

This is the 3rd edition of the Visitor's Guide to Bermuda. It has been updated; more pictures have been added, some have been enlarged for better viewing, as have the maps, and the paperback version is now has 244 pages.

Bermuda is not a single island at all, but a great, fishhook-shaped atoll of more than 180 small islands and islets surrounded by the deep blue waters of the Atlantic Ocean. Bermuda is a magical place located some 600 miles to the east of Cape Hatteras on the coast of the United States.. It's an island I fell in love with more years ago than I care to remember. What I do remember is that first flight in over the reef: the turquoise blue of the deep ocean, the emerald shallows, and the verdant greens, pastel colors and glistening whites on the islands proper. Magical does not describe that first glimpse of Bermuda from the air.

Photo Courtesy of the Bermuda Department of Tourism

Bermuda is a quiet world of pastel-colored buildings with snowy-white roofs, turquoise shallows and pale pink beaches. Whether it's the combination of the English culture and its quasi-tropical setting, or something else, Bermuda is, in my opinion, one of the most beautiful places on Earth. There's something very special about this little group of islands. I've lost count of the number of times I've visited the island; it's addictive, an experience you'll never forget.

Hamilton, the islands' tiny capital city is set on the shores of the Great Sound, is a microcosm of a quasi-English culture that's something of an anomaly: the little shops, churches and cafes on narrow streets might well have plucked from any one of a hundred little English towns; the old-word cathedral, the bright red British pillar boxes (post boxes), and the food, especially afternoon tea - an almost religious experience in Bermuda - all seem to make Bermuda even more British than England itself. Nowhere in England, however, will you find anything that can compare to the pink sandy beaches, the crystal waters, or the beautiful island terrain.

Today, Bermuda welcomes visitors from around the world; every budget is catered for. You can spend a week, or two, or more at one of the expensive luxury resort hotels, or perhaps one of small cottage colonies; you can stay at one of a hundred neat little bed & breakfast homes, guest houses, all-inclusive hotels, or you might like to choose from one of the many self-catering options. Whatever your budget might be, you're sure to find something to suit your taste, and your wallet. You can do six nights, seven days on the islands for as little as $1,250 U.S. per person, or you can pay that much, or more, per night. Whatever your budget, you're sure of a grand time.

Geography

Bermuda is located some 600 miles to the east of Cape Hatteras. Bermuda is, to say the least, isolated. That being said, Bermuda is one of the World's most popular tourist destinations. No more than a tiny dot on most of the maps, if it shows at all, we have to wonder how the explorers of more than five centuries ago managed to find it at all.

Bermuda is an atoll set upon the peaks of a volcano. An underwater mountain, many thousands of feet high, with slopes that rise from depths of the ocean to a point about 200 feet below the surface of the Atlantic. Above this level, the islands rise out of the sea, great slabs of limestone formed by seashells and corals. The shoreline, surrounded by those famous pink beaches, and sculpted over thousands of years by the ocean and ever-present winds, is an improbable world of grottoes, caves, giant off-shore rocks and boilers; it's world that might have right out of the imagination of J. R. R. Tolkien .

Seen from space, the Islands of Bermuda, look somewhat like a fishhook, with the hook and barb at the southwest end and the eye to the northeast. As you fly in over the island, the view is stunning, a green, green landscape splashed with a myriad of eye-catching colors, and all surrounded by sparkling blue waters.

Homes, churches, shops and even sheds, painted in pastel shades of pink, blue, green, yellow and all the other colors of the rainbow, are capped with snowy white roofs. The islands are a patchwork quilt, thrown down in the middle of the blue ocean.

The reefs surrounding the Bermuda, and the islands themselves, are made mostly of coral, and the Bermudian archipelago is the northernmost point on the planet that supports its growth. Coral stone is Bermuda's one great natural resource. It provides Bermuda with stone for road-building and construction material. The coral stone in its natural state is so soft it can be cut with handsaws; once cut, however, it soon hardens with exposure to air. Bermuda's glistening white roads are nothing more than coral bedrock stripped, smoothed and then allowed to harden.

Traditional Bermuda Roof

Those famous, white tiered roofs, unique to Bermuda, are also built of coral stone. Legend has it that the roofs are designed to resemble upturned lifeboats, perhaps the first shelters of the mariners we know were shipwrecked on the islands more than 500 years ago. Today, the roofs serve a second and very important purpose: the unique structure of the Bermuda roof is designed to catch rainwater, the islands' chief source of drinking water. Bermuda has no rivers or fresh-water lakes. That being so most of the island's fresh arrives in the form of rain which is channeled from the roofs into underground cisterns – every private home has one.

The Bermudian archipelago has a total land mass of less than 22 square miles. Only 20 of the islands are inhabited. The 10 largest are joined together by a series of bridges and scenic causeways. The ocean is ever-present, and can be seen from almost anywhere. The Main Island, Great Bermuda, is larger than all the other islands combined. At its highest point, Town Hill, rises some 260 feet above sea level.

The community is divided into nine parishes, each managed by an advisory council: Sandy's Parish, Southampton, Warwick, Paget, Devonshire, Pembroke, Smiths, Hamilton, and St. George's.

The Climate

The climate, for the most part, is delightful. The average mean temperature is 70°F. In winter time, the temperatures rarely drop below 55°; in summer time, they rarely go above 87°.

Rainfall can be heavy at times - almost 60 inches annually. That, accompanied by an average of eight hours of sunshine 315 days per year, guarantees an abundance of lush vegetation: palms, casuarinas and swamp mangroves are among the common trees. Hibiscus, oleander, poinsettia, and many other flowering plants and trees bloom profusely. Easter lilies are cultivated for export and are also used to make perfumes.

More than 200 species of birds have been catalogued on the islands (although most of them are migratory birds blown off course); and that reminds me a funny, but somewhat tragic story, but we'll keep that for another day.

The waters off Bermuda are warm, or warmish, the year round, and literally teem with fish, many of which are remarkable for their striking colors and markings. The waters in-shore are clear waters with good visibility up to 200 feet and beyond.

About Hurricanes

There's no doubt that hurricanes can be a factor when considering a visit to Bermuda. It is, after all, a low-lying island group and subject, though not so often as you might imagine to hurricane force winds and rain.

Hurricane season runs from June through November, but Bermuda has been lucky for many years. Big winds do blow, but most hurricanes seem to skirt the island. Tropical storms with winds of up to 75 miles an hour can make for an exciting day or two. The architecture on the islands, though, is built to withstand all but the most intense category five hurricanes. Interestingly, the islanders always seem to know instinctively, well in advance, when there's a "big blow" coming. Apparently it has something to do with the activities of insects and spiders, birds, the atmosphere, and even the action of the sea on the South Shore.

Hurricane Categories

Atlantic hurricanes are ranked by the Saffir-Simpson hurricane intensity scale to give an estimate of the potential flooding and damage. Category three and above is considered intense.

Category Winds (mph) Damage

Category One 74-95 Minimal: Damage primarily to shrubbery, trees and foliage.

Category Two 96-110 Moderate: Considerable damage to shrubbery and foliage; some trees blown down. Some damage to roofing materials.

Category Three 111-130 Extensive: Foliage torn from trees; large trees blown down. Some structural damage to small buildings. Mobile homes destroyed. Flooding along the coastline.

Category Four 131-155 Extreme: Shrubs and trees blown down. Complete failure of roofs on small residences. Major beach erosion. Massive evacuation of all homes within 500 yards of shore possibly required.

Category Five 155 Catastrophic: Some complete building failures. Small buildings overturned or blown away. Low-lying escape routes inland cut by rising water three to five hours before the hurricane's center arrives.

The Attractions

Bermuda is one of the smallest countries in the world, even so the little island nation offers plenty to see and do: If you love the great outdoors, there are hiking trails to explore, diving, snorkeling, sport fishing, exploring, sailing, windsurfing, golfing, shopping, tennis, island hopping and parasailing.

Do you enjoy sightseeing? If so, there are great military forts to visit, fine old churches, magnificent lighthouses, historic buildings, botanical gardens, a national aquarium, museums and the great Royal Naval Dockyard at the West End of the island. As you tour the islands, you'll travel through one tiny town after another: neat, pastel-colored homes with snowy white roofs and beautifully maintained English gardens full of hibiscus, oleander and Bermudiana.

The Old Prison at the Royal Naval Dockyard

The outlying areas, if you could really call them that, are dotted with tiny farms that grow crops of tomatoes, sweet potatoes, onions and other vegetables. Bananas hang heavily from trees in great green and yellow bunches. Magnificent pink beaches, green golf courses and the eye-popping turquoise ocean combine to create a tropical utopia. And with 12 nature reserves on the Main Island alone, Bermuda is also a haven for naturalists.

The City of Hamilton is the capital and chief port of Bermuda. Located in Pembroke Parish on the Main Island, Hamilton covers a total area of less 200 acres, that and its small population of only 2,000, makes it one of the world's smallest cities.

The City of St. George is located at the East End of the group on St. George's Island and is Bermuda's second city. A picturesque little port, St. George is one of Bermuda's oldest settlements.

The Population

Bermuda is home to about 65,000 people, 65% of them are black. Although Bermuda's heritage is basically British, its people have, over the past 300 years or so, been heavily influenced by its semi-tropical location. And, while the average Bermudian is very British, the Caribbean influence and its African roots, have had a real effect on its culture. The colorful clothing and many of the important festivals reflect beginnings born in slavery. Caribbean music - the sounds of the steel bands, reggae and calypso - wafts gently across the islands, bringing with it a feeling of well-being and a decidedly happy-go-lucky attitude.

Daily life on Bermuda is much the same as it is in England. Darts are played in pubs; fish and chips, sausage rolls, and meat pies are on most menus; and afternoon tea is a tradition that's inviolable – oh yes, everything stops for tea.

On a tiny island like this one, no place is exclusive just to the locals - where they go, you go. And, as most of the people use the public transportation system – the buses – inevitably, you'll find yourself in close contact with the residents; you'll find it fun, too.

Photo Courtesy of the Bermuda Department of Tourism

The average Bermudian is friendly, sometimes almost to fault; easy to like and easy to get to know. Bermudians will strike up a conversation with visitors anytime, anywhere, on buses, the ferry, in pubs or on the beach. If you need help, you have only to ask. The average Bermudian is well educated and extremely articulate. You'll have no trouble understanding them.

The Economy

Despite its isolation, lack of manufacturing industry and a cost of living that ranks among the highest in the world, Bermuda has almost no poverty or unemployment. There is no income tax, nor does the government receive any foreign aid.

Tourism is king in Bermuda. Each year more than 600,000 tourists – most of them from the US and Canada – visit the islands; thus tourism accounts for about 40 of the colony's total income. Banking and insurance are second only to tourism.

Bermuda still adheres very to its British traditions; the influence of the Royal Navy is still felt, even today. The pubs are, these days, even more British than those in the UK. The fish and chips are much the same in Hamilton as they are/were in London, and more often than not, even better; cricket is Bermuda's national sport, and tea is served every afternoon at four o'clock. The Queen's English is often spoken, especially by whites, with a clipped, upper-class accent.

History

From the dawn of its history, more than 500 years ago, Bermuda has been an island of adventure. Explorers, opportunists, castaways, and rovers of just about every European nationality have made a home, or at least a base, on these islands.

It was on a calm and pleasant day in 1503, when Juan de Bermudez, a Spanish explorer, became the first European to set foot on the islands, though not by choice, so the story goes. And thus, after several changes, including "Isle of Devils" and the "Somers Isles," the islands got their name. Senor Bermudez was shortly followed by several more erstwhile Spanish explorers. Due to the seemingly interminably bad weather, and the decidedly unfriendly nature of the shoreline, no one bothered to claim the islands for Spain.

Six years later, in 1609, an English ship bound for Jamestown was shipwrecked off what is now St. Catherine's Point. The Sea Venture, commanded by Sir George Somers, went onto the reef with 150 souls on board, including John Rolfe, who later married the Indian Princess, Pocahontas; Sir Thomas Gates, the Deputy Governor of Jamestown; and Christopher Newport, the leader of the first expedition to Jamestown.

These were the first English visitors to the island, again not really by choice.

Replica of the Sea Venture

Fortunately, everyone on the Sea Venture made it safely ashore. What was left of the Sea Venture, was quickly salvaged and two ships were built from the recovered timbers and sails; The adventurers then set sail once more for Jamestown. In the meantime, Sir George claimed the islands for England, and they have remained a British colony ever since.

But that's not the end of the story. When Sir George and his ships finally made it to Jamestown, he found that most of the colonists had died. The winter of 1609-1610 had been so bad, that it became known as the "Starving Time." Somers unloaded his two small ships and immediately put to sea and headed back to Bermuda in search of food for the starving colony. Unfortunately, Sir George died in Bermuda. His companions buried his heart in a memorial garden established by the survivors of the wreck of the Sea Venture; his body was shipped back to England. Following Sir George's death, Bermuda became known as the Somers Isles, a name which, even today, is not uncommon among Bermudians.

Sir George Somers

In 1612, the first group of permanent settlers on the islands established the city of St. George near St. Catherine's Point. In 1620, the British Colonial Government was founded, a Royal Governor was appointed, and a legislature was established in St. George. In 1684 a new parliament was established, and Bermuda has been a self-governing British colony ever since. For more than 200 years, St. George was the capital of Bermuda. In 1815, the capital was moved to Hamilton where it has remained ever since.

Holidays

Bermudians enjoy their life on this semi-tropical paradise, and they enjoy their holidays even more. Any excuse is good enough for public party, and for the gombay dancers to don their colorful garb and dance through the city streets, especially on such public holidays as Boxing Day (December 26th), New Year's Day, Good Friday, Easter Monday, and during May (Heritage Month), and any other special day. Gombay is the African word for drum or rhythm, the tradition was born of slavery and is celebrated, in one form or another, throughout the Caribbean and the West Indies.

The gaily gaily-colored, the feathered headdresses, elaborate costumes, fantastically carved masks, are a sight to behold; the acrobatic leaping, gyrating dancing, and throbbing island music are hypnotic. If, by chance, you should visit during one of these special holidays, you'll likely find yourself dancing to the beat, along with a host of locals, and following the parade as it meanders slowly through back and forth through the city streets.

Photo Courtesy of the Bermuda Department of Tourism

As I mentioned earlier, Bermuda's national sport is cricket (what else could it be?) and, the annual grudge match played between St. George and Somerset, is perhaps the strongest of the island traditions. The Cup Match, a two-day event, was born at the turn of the 20th century to celebrate Sir George Somers and the abolition of slavery. And grudge match it is; visitors find it difficult to believe that a cricket match could stir up so much emotion. Rivalry between the two teams, and their parent communities, is obsessive. The match is played either in late July or early August. Now, just as the cricket match is the center of the celebration, socializing is just as important. The event brings intense competition on the field, along with wild island music, dancing, food, and much more. If you can make it to Bermuda for the Cup Match, you're in for a treat.

Travel Information

When to Go

Peak Season

The high season – April through September – is the best time to visit Bermuda. The weather, events, activities and attractions are all at their peak. All of the beaches are open – and they can be crowded at times, especially on weekends - and there are organized tours, barbecues, cricket matches and evening entertainment options.

Summer days in Bermuda are balmy, the evenings warm and romantic, and the nights are cool. Daytime temperatures rise into the mid-80s to low 90s; in the evenings they range from highs in the mid-60s to the low 70s. When it rains, it does so mostly in the evenings, sometimes heavily. Rain is extremely important to Bermuda; there is no other natural source of water on the island, so the occasional gully washer is always welcomed: it fills up the storage tanks.

Off Season

Bermuda's off season includes the months from November through February. Now, to me, the off season is the best time to visit. First, and perhaps most important, it costs significantly less. As to the weather, well, the climate is always temperate; yes, it's cooler which can make for a more comfortable visit, but not so cold as to be uncomfortable. The beaches, shops and hotels are less crowded, and life on the island, slow even at peak times, drops another notch. The swimming, diving, hiking and fishing are just as good – perhaps even more enjoyable with the lack of tourists.

Photo Courtesy of the Bermuda Department of Tourism

Now, having said all that, you should also be aware that many popular attractions, restaurants, museums and hotels close, or at least operate on reduced hours during off season. If you a golf lover, it's a good time to visit Bermuda. The cooler weather makes golf and tennis that much more enjoyable. Then there are a number of special events and walking tours organized especially for Bermuda's winter visitors. This, too, is a good reason to visit during the off season.

If you can book your vacation during the off season, you're likely to get a good deal. The hotels usually offer reduced rates than can be as much as 40lower than those in the peak season; they need to fill the empty space.

If you're anything like me, you'll just love the solitude that you can find during the winter months in Bermuda: seemingly isolated, windswept beaches; cool sea breezes, quiet streets and shops, It's a good time to visit. I've made several visits in the off-season and I always have a good time. Daytime temperatures are in the high 60s to low 70s most of the time, and there's more than enough to see and do to keep you busy. You will, however, need to take a warm jacket for the evenings and a light sweater in case it gets chilly during the day.

How to Get There

Getting to Bermuda is just about as easy as it can get. Almost all major U.S. and Canadian airlines offer service from most of the larger cities. The United Kingdom, too, is also well-served by both British and American airlines, although most American carrier are routed through one of the hubs on the American mainland.

Bermuda is also on the itinerary of most cruise lines, most of them now very attractive rates.

All-inclusive package vacations offer another attractive option, and there are a growing number of companies in the US, Canada and Europe ready to compete for your business. Package tour operators may be the airlines themselves or independent companies, each offering a variety of products designed to suit every budget. JetBlue, British Airways, American Airlines Vacations, Delta Vacations, and US Airways Vacations, all offer reasonably-priced vacation packages to Bermuda.

Vacation Planning Online

Over the many years I've been traveling the world I've booked extensive trips by myself; I've used travel agents and, over the last ten years or so, I've used a variety of Internet providers. Yes, there are bargains to be found online, you just have to know where to look. Before you decide to go it alone, however, there are a couple of things you should know: not only do you often get precisely what you pay for; you might just find you get a lot less. For instance, whom do you appeal to when things go wrong? And they may. A good travel agent will often have first-hand knowledge of many of the popular resorts and will be able to recommend good hotels and restaurants.

Better yet, the same travel agent may be able to steer you away from the traps. He/she will be able to provide trip insurance, day trips and itineraries. In short, a good travel agent will ensure you get value for money and real back-up when you need it. But, if you're determined to go it alone, I recommend you use only well-established companies, such as Hotels.com, Expedia.com, Orbitz.com and Travelocity.com.

These sites cater to the true "independent" traveler. Here you can book airline tickets, hotels and rental cars – often at a discount. If you've not used a direct booking service before, make sure you understand exactly what you're buying: are there any restrictions on your airline tickets? Can you cancel or are they nonrefundable?

If there are restrictions, you need to know what penalties would apply if you needed to cancel close to the departure date? You should understand that a cheap airline ticket almost always means there are restrictions. Second, be sure to shop around; there's always a better deal no more than a couple of clicks away. Third, don't forget such websites as hotels.com, hotelclub.com and hoteldiscounts.com. Combine an inexpensive airline ticket with a discounted hotel stay and you should have a total cost you can live with.

Most of the major airlines, and some package operators have websites. Many, if not all, of the advantages of using an online booking agent are available at these sites. Delta Airlines, American Airlines, USAir, and many more, all offer extensive package options that include airfare, car rental, hotel rooms, trip insurance, and airport/hotels transfers, often at big discounts (depending upon when you want to go).

These companies are very good at what they do. They have inspectors visiting resorts on a regular basis to make sure that things are just as they should be. They own the airline, which means if a flight is cancelled you are their first priority for the next available flight. True, you might run into a small hitch here and there but, on the whole, you can rest assured that what you pay for is exactly what you get. And it's true one-stop-shopping. A few clicks and you're done. If you want to book online yourself, I think this is the way to go.

Additional Travel Websites

Most independent package tour operators, such as Vacation Express and Travel Impressions, prefer that you book your vacation through a travel agent. The theory is that they have less trouble dealing with an agent, with whom they will already have built a long-term relationship, than they do when dealing directly with the general public. Even so, many will deal with you directly, but only online. For that reason, most operators, including the airline vacation companies, prefer not to publish phone numbers.

By Air
Commercial Airlines

Commercial airlines serving Bermuda include Air Canada (888-247-2262), American Airlines (800-433-7300), British Airways (_800-247-9297), Continental (800-231-0856), Delta (800-221-1212) and US Airways (800-622-1015), many with direct flights from Atlanta, Baltimore, Boston, London, Miami, New York, Newark, Raleigh/Durham and Toronto. Of these, Delta offers the most comprehensive service and the most convenient schedule of flights (with direct, non-stop flights from both Atlanta and Boston). American Airlines offers a complete non-stop flight schedule departing from New York and Boston, often at the best rates.

Important Note: airline passengers cannot transport luggage on the Bermuda Public Transport buses. You will need to use the airport shuttle service or hire a taxi to get to your hotel.

Private Aircraft

Private aircraft are permitted to fly into Bermuda International Airport. However, the government requires that all private and commercial air traffic make arrangements for ground handling with an approved agency on the islands. Bermuda Aviation Service Ltd. can be reached at 441-293-2500, by radio on VHF 131.6 MHz, or by mail at PO Box HM 718, Hamilton, Bermuda HM CX. Or try Mid-Atlantic Aviation Ltd., _441-293-4622, VHF 131.65 MHz, or PO Box 11, Bermuda, GE CX. These two agencies will act as representatives for you, your crew and passengers, handling all customs and immigration procedures, documentation, hanger facilities, aircraft services and ground transportation.

Cruise Ships

Bermuda is, perhaps, the ultimate cruise destination, especially from the United States. Arriving cruise ships dock either at the Royal Naval Dockyard or at St. George's. From either port, getting around is easy. The ferries run convenient services between the Royal Naval Dockyard and Hamilton, and they also serve Paget, Warwick and Somerset counties.

Photo Courtesy of the Bermuda Department of Tourism

Using the ferry is fun and inexpensive; the service is frequent convenient. You'll find ferry schedules at the end of this Guide.

If you are visiting Bermuda by cruise ship, all of your wants and needs will be supplied on-board ship, and most of what you'll consume (meals, snacks, soft drinks at the table) is included in the package price. The only extras are souvenirs, day trips at ports of call, and your flight (if necessary) to get you to your port of departure. Most often the best airfares can be found through the cruise lines themselves.

All major cruise lines book block space on aircraft departing from all major airline hubs such as New York, Chicago, Atlanta, Miami, and Charlotte. Connector flights however – those providing transport between your hometown and the airline's hub – will run the airfare up appreciably.

Accommodations on-board range from cramped, windowless cubicles deep in the bowels of the ship, to large, luxury suites on an upper deck, complete with balcony, lots of space to spread out, and all modern conveniences – even butler service.

Note: I have cruised to Bermuda a couple of times, and my advice is that you book a mid-priced outside stateroom. You'll have a little more room than in cheaper staterooms, a view of the ocean and port of call as you arrive and leave, and the rate is not that much more.

Once on board, you can visit the ship's pursers and they will, should you so desire, arrange a variety of day trips and fun things to do – activities such as scuba diving, snorkeling and windsurfing, to name a few. You can also rent motor scooters to explore the island. My advice, though, is to book through your travel agent whatever you think you'll need or want to do before you leave. If you wait until you're on board, it's first-come, first-served, and you may not get what you want. If you do decide to leave it until you get on board, book as soon as you can.

If you're on a tight budget, you can save money booking tours, daytrips and/or activities independently, outside of the cruise line, at one of the Tourist Information Centers in Hamilton or at the Royal Naval Dockyard. Since the cruise lines make a profit on offered extras, you'll pay less, and you may find you have a whole more options to choose from. Once again, your travel agent may be able to help. If not, use the phone numbers listed in this book.

Cruising to Bermuda is not an inexpensive vacation; there are no two or three-nighters, like there are to the Bahamas. Most cruises to Bermuda last for six or seven nights, with at least three nights spent on the island. Sometimes a cruise special can be found for as little as $850 per person, not including airfare to the port of departure. Without a special, and at peak travel times, you may well find yourself paying at least double that.

Of all the cruise lines serving Bermuda, Celebrity – now a part of the Royal Caribbean Cruise Line – usually offers the least expensive options. At the high end, cruising is still regarded as a very special experience and you can expect to pay upward of $4,000 per person. If it's luxury and formality you're looking for, such cruise lines as Cunard and Crystal can provide that once-in-a-lifetime cruising experience. Whatever the price range or cruise line you choose, however, you can expect to be well looked after – all food and snacks are provided, along with soft drinks at the table. Most cruise lines now charge for soft drinks at the pool and for ice cream. Beer, wine and liquor are not included in the cost of most cruises; you'll pay an additional cost for those (at prices that will often bring on sticker-shock).

But cruising is a great way to visit Bermuda, as it is to visit any exotic location. Long, lazy days on deck, lounging poolside, being waited on hand and foot every waking moment, makes cruising an unforgettable experience. Feel like really pampering yourself? The spa and salon are only a deck away. Tropical sea breezes, watching the moon rise over the ocean, with the trackless sea stretching to the horizon in every direction – these are moments you can experience no other way.

The Food on Board

No matter the cruise line, the food is always a little out of the ordinary. On most ships, the menu, cuisine and the overall standard of excellence is looked after by a master chef, and the food is always special Afternoon tea is usually the afternoon highlight and includes homemade, freshly-baked scones with strawberry jam and clotted cream. The midnight buffets, extravaganzas of goodies where all-you-can-eat is the watchword, are also a rather special experience. Want to dine in your room? No problem. Order room service from the menu or have gourmet pizza delivered to your door. The dining rooms are large, airy and offer grand views of the ocean

Paying for Extras on Board

You'll be expected to provide a credit card number or to prepay for a ship-board charge card. This means you'll hand over several hundred dollars (or British pounds), and they'll give you a credit account for charging all your extras. (Don't worry, they let you know as soon as your credit is up and you need to give them some more money.) It's easy to run up your bill. Several rounds of drinks will hit you hard, and you may lose track when you're having a good time.

Casinos on Board

Be very careful, If you lose all your money on the outward-bound leg of the cruise.... A vacation with little or no spending money can be a harrowing experience.

A Typical Cruise Schedule

The following gives you an idea of a Bermuda cruise schedule. Celebrity's Zenith cruises to Bermuda from New York 28 times each year, from early May through the end of October. The itinerary at the time of writing was as follows:

Saturday: Depart New York 4:30 pm

Sunday: At sea
Monday: Arrive Hamilton, Bermuda at 8 am
Tuesday: Hamilton
Wednesday: Depart Hamilton at 6 am
Wednesday: Arrive St. George at 9 am
Thursday: Depart St. George at 3 pm
Friday: At sea
Saturday: Arrive New York at 8 am

Rates start at around $1,049 and rise to more than $2,200 depending upon the season and cabin.

Cruise Lines

Bermuda is served by:

Celebrity Cruises, 877-202-4345 or www.celebritycruises.com
Norwegian Cruise Line, 866-625-1166 or www.nd.com
Royal Caribbean Cruises, Ltd., 866-562-7625 or www.royalcaribbean.com

Rates range from $599 to $1729.

Private Yacht

For the sea-going adventurer, sailing to Bermuda under your own steam, or sail, is a great way to go, if you have a vessel big enough and sturdy enough to make the journey.

The weather is obviously an important factor when making sail for Bermuda. The hurricane season – June through November – brings untold hazards, and December through April can be equally harrowing due to sudden storms and high winds that strike with little or no warning.

Bermuda's port of entry for all visiting yachts and small vessels is St. George's. All crew members and passengers must clear Customs and Immigration.

There's a 24-hour facility on Ordnance Island, St. George's, but if you arrive after dark, it might be best to wait until dawn before entering port. To approach port, you must contact Bermuda Harbour Radio and give your ETA. The facility listens 24 hours a day on 2182 Khz USB and on VHF 16 (distress channel). Use these channels only for contacting Bermuda Harbour Radio.

All passengers and crew, including for US and Canadian citizens, are required to have valid a passport.

If you plan to stay more than a week and live on board your boat, all Bermudian health regulations must be complied with. Notify the Department of Marine and Ports of your plans. They will then supply you with a copy of the regulations. Contact them after clearing Customs and Immigration. 441-295-6575.

Important Note: The rates for docking listed below were correct at the time of writing. Please remember, however, that all are subject to change at a moment's notice and you should check with the provider for current rates before you go.

Navigable Bridge

The swing bridge between Ferry Reach and Castle Harbour (above) is opened upon request from 7:30 am to 7 pm, daily, April through September, and 7:30 am to 5 pm, October through March. If you intend to make sail from St. George's to Hamilton, this route can cut as much as 30 minutes from the normal two-hour sail, and make it more interesting. Contact the Department of Marine & Ports, 441-295-6575.

Marinas

St. George's

Captain Smokes Marina, McCallan's Wharf 13, Wellington St., Town of St. George. _441-297-1940. Fresh water, 110- and 220-volt electrical hookups, fuel.

Photo Courtesy of the Bermuda Department of Tourism

Sandy's Parish

This comprises four small islands at the western end of the archipelago. Among other attractions, you'll find the Royal Naval Dockyard and Maritime Museum housed in what was once the largest fortress on the island. Together, the fortress and the Dockyard comprised one of the most important strongholds of the British Navy during the 18th and 19th centuries.

Today, the West End is a tourist attraction; it's also home to the Dockyard Marina. Dockyard Marina, 9 Dockyard Terrace, Royal Naval Dockyard, Ireland Island, Bermuda. 441-234-0300. The marina is housed within the confines of the Dockyard breakwater. Facilities include fresh water, fuel and a clubhouse. Daily, weekly and monthly rates are available.

Hamilton

Hamilton Royal Bermuda Yacht Club, Albouy's Port, Hamilton, Bermuda. 441-295-2214. As its name implies, the Royal Bermuda Yacht Club holds a royal

Warrant granted by Queen Elizabeth II and has held such warrants continuously since the reign of Queen Victoria. What does this mean to you, the erstwhile mariner from across the ocean? Not much, I'm afraid. It does mean that it's a very exclusive club, with memberships received more on inheritance than application. Still, you can take advantage of the club's berths and services simply by tying up and registering. An account will be opened, allowing you and your crew full advantage of most of what's available. The club is situated on Albouy's Point in the city – all the sights and sounds of Hamilton are close at hand. Vessel size is limited to 80 feet maximum.

If you are indeed going to sail to Bermuda, consider buying a copy of The Bermuda Yachting Guide. This extremely informative book, published by the Bermuda Maritime Museum Association, provides most of the information you'll need during your stay in the islands, including anchorages. In the US, purchase it from Blue water Books and Charts, 1481 SE 17th Street Causeway, Ft. Lauderdale, FL 33316, www.bluewaterweb.com. Or order it direct from the publisher, Bermuda Maritime Museum Association, PO Box MA 273, Mangrove Bay, MA BX, Bermuda. 441-234-1333.

Passports & Visas

Americans & Canadians: You'll need a round-trip or onward ticket and a valid passport. Passports can be obtained by US citizens through your local post office; allow up to 12 weeks when applying.

Citizens of the United Kingdom: You'll need a valid passport for visits of up to 30 days.

Bermuda Department of Tourism

In the United States, for brochures and automated information, 800-237-6832 or visit www.bermudatourism.com. You can call or write the Bermuda Department of Tourism office at 205 E. 42nd Street, New York, NY 10017; 212-818-9800.

In Canada, contact the Bermuda Department of Tourism at 1200 Bay Street, Suite 1004, Toronto, ON, Canada M5R 2A5; 416-923-9600.In the United Kingdom, contact the Bermuda Department of Tourism at 1 Battersea Church Road, London, SW11 3lY; 020-8410-8188.

Never pack your passport in your checked luggage!

Customs & Duties

Here's one you may not know about. If you own an expensive camera, watch or electronic equipment, register it with customs officials at your home port or airport of departure. This will eliminate any import problems you might encounter on your return. You may take into Bermuda duty-free: 50 cigars, 200 cigarettes, one pound of tobacco, one quart of liquor and one quart of wine.

Returning home, US citizens may take up to $400 worth of goods, duty-free; Canadian citizens, $300; and citizens of the United Kingdom, £390.

US Customs pre-clearance is available for all US residents returning on scheduled flights.

You must pay a departure tax of $20 per person before leaving Bermuda.

Trip Insurance

Do you need it? Yes, I think you do. It's not only prudent to be well-insured, it's smart. First, medical attention is expensive and, secondly, if you have to cancel your trip or if it's canceled due to the bankruptcy or default of one or more of your operators, that can be expensive too.

Before buying extra insurance, check to see what your existing medical and homeowner's insurance policies cover. Most major medical policies cover at least medical and dental emergencies. If not, ask your agent to make the necessary changes.

Traveling with Children

Bermuda has never been regarded as a family vacation destination. Activities and amenities are still very much adult-oriented. Other than the sea and the sand, there's little for children to do. Most major resorts and some of the smaller hotels now offer children's programs, and some provide baby-sitting services. The going rate for these services is around $7 per hour, and if you have to bring in someone from the outside, you'll be expected to pay round-trip transportation.

Be sure to check the hotel's policy before you book – some hotels do not allow children on the premises.

Disabled Travelers

Bermuda can challenge the physically handicapped, especially when traveling around the island. The majority of large resort hotels are accessible to handicapped visitors; most of the smaller ones are not. Many of the larger shops and stores cater to the handicapped traveler, but smaller ones do not.

Important Note: The Pink and Blue public buses are NOT equipped to handle wheelchairs, but the ferries can handle them quite easily.

The Bermuda Physically Handicapped Association does, however, have a bus with a hydraulic lift. It's operated by volunteers, and you can make arrangements in advance by writing Box HM 08, Hamilton, Bermuda HM AX, or 441-292-5025.

Visually-impaired persons wanting to travel with a guide dog must apply for a permit prior to travel. Once this is granted, it must be carried with you at all times. Applications are available at any of the Bermuda Tourism Offices listed below.

Bermuda Information Offices

The Bermuda Department of Tourism can be reached through its offices in the following locations:

Bermuda: Global House, 43 Church St., Hamilton, HM 12, Bermuda, 800-BERMUDA, www.bermudatourism.com.

New York: 205 E. 42nd St., New York, NY 10017, 800-223-6106 or 212-818-9800.

Atlanta: 245 Peachtree Center Avenue NE, Suite 803, Atlanta, GA 30303, 404-524-1541.

Canada: 1200 Bay Street, Suite 1004, Toronto, Ontario, M5R 2A5, _800-387-1304 or 416-923-9600.

London: Bermuda Tourism, BCB Ltd., 1 Battersea Church Road, London, SW11 3LY, 020-8410-8188 or 020-7866-9924.

Money

The Bermuda dollar is divided into 100 cents, and is pegged, through gold, to the American dollar. The US dollar is accepted by all merchants on the islands; change will often be given as a mixture of American and Bermudian currency. Cash machines are also widely available.

Checks

Personal checks drawn on US banks may be used for purchases at more than 200 locations. US checks can be cashed at some hotels or at local banks by arrangement. The Bermuda Financial Network at 441-292-1799 will cash US checks for a 3 fee. US traveler's checks are accepted island-wide.

Credit Cards

MasterCard, Visa and American Express are accepted at virtually every store, restaurant and hotel and may be used for cash advances at all local bank branches.

ATMs

ATMs are provided at locations island-wide by the Bank of Bermuda and the Bank of Butterfield. They accept MasterCard, Visa, Cirrus and Plus, and are available for advances 24 hours a day. The Bermuda Financial Network at 441-292-1799 will provide assistance to visitors who need help with American Express.

Need money from home fast? There's a Western Union location in the City of Hamilton at the Gibbons Deposit Company. You can contact them at 441-296-6969.

Costs

Although it seems that almost everything in Bermuda is expensive, you'll receive excellent value for your money. Accommodations in the summer season can run anywhere from $100 a night at a small hotel to as high as $450. During the winter, however, rates drop considerably. The low-season rates at many of the guest houses begin at around $75, and a room at a bed & breakfast might go for as little as $50 per night, including breakfast. You'll have to share a bathroom, but the personal service and friendly atmosphere can make it quite a bargain for those on a budget.

Note: Many of the island's small hotels and guest houses do not take credit cards.

Hotel & Restaurant Prices

Throughout the book restaurant prices are indicated as follows:

Restaurant Price Scale:

$$$+ Over $50 per person

$$ $20-$50 per person

$ Under $25 per person

Hotel Price Scale

$$$$ More than $250 per night

$$$ $150-$250 per night

$$ $100-$150 per night

$ Less than $100 per night

Some of the quoted hotel rates might be subject to an energy surcharge. All rates are subject to a 7.25hotel occupancy tax and do not include gratuities.

Meal Plans at Hotels Most hotels offer a choice between MAP, BP or EP rates. Guest houses usually offer a choice of BP, CP or EP.

CP (Continental Plan): provides a continental breakfast.

EP (European Plan): denotes no set meal plan, although restaurant facilities are either on the property or nearby.

BP (Bermudian Plan): offers room and full breakfast.

MAP (Modified American Plan): includes breakfast and dinner.

FAP (Full American Plan): includes all meals.

Tipping

Be sure to read your bill before you tip. Many restaurants will automatically add a 15 service charge. If you don't see it, ask before you tip. Your hotel will add a 10 service charge to the rate. This covers everything from maid service to the dining room to the hotel porter, so there's no need to leave a room tip. Porters and baggage handlers at the airport expect to receive a dollar per bag, and cab drivers usually receive 15of the fare.

Golf & Tennis

Green fees at the golf courses can range from a low of $49 to a high of $280.

Tennis, too, is reasonable. Most hotels allow paying guests to use their courts free of charge. Visitors, however, will be required to register and pay by the hour – anywhere from $6 to $15, depending on the establishment.

Photo Courtesy of the Bermuda Department of Tourism

When in Rome... Bermuda

Bermudans are of the old British school: they are big on good manners and mutual respect. Bad language in public is very much frowned upon. They will definitely be a little put out if approached and questioned without so much as a hello or good morning. When interacting with waiters, store clerks and anyone else in public service, always look them in the eye, pay attention to what they're saying, and talk directly to them; it's all a part of good manners. In Bermuda, gentlemen still give up their seats to ladies when traveling on a crowded bus. Remain seated while a lady has to stand, and you're sure to garner a scornful look or two.

Clothing & Dress

Bermudians are also a little old-fashioned about their dress code, what's acceptable and what's not. Scanty dress is also unacceptable: do NOT wear bikini tops and skimpy shorts on city streets; it will receive a friendly warning from the local bobby. Men, if you wear shorts in public, and who doesn't these days? They should not be cut much higher than an inch above the knee. A shirt should always be worn in public. Casual sportswear is accepted everywhere.

About Bermuda shorts: The famous short pants, traditional to the island, are still worn by local men in every walk of life. These "long shorts" were introduced to the islands by British military personnel around the turn of the century. Today, especially during the summer, you'll see policemen, complete with English bobby's hat and Bermuda shorts, directing traffic or ticketing speeders. Bankers wearing business suits with a white shirt, conservative tie, "trousers" an inch above the knee, tall socks above the calf, and a pair of highly polished shoes, is the norm, and can be a little surprising at first.

Photo Courtesy of the Bermuda Department of Tourism

In the evenings you'll need to dress more formally. Ladies can wear a cocktail dress, and a suit and tie is required for men at most restaurants and hotel dining rooms. Winter evenings can also be a little cool so, if you like to walk, pack a light sweater or jacket.

Tennis players must dress properly on all courts. This means white shorts or white tennis shirts, and white socks and tennis shoes.

Proper attire is also required on golf courses. Shorts must be of Bermuda length, cut just above the knee, and shirts must have collars. No jeans, gym shorts or cut-offs are allowed.

Medical Services

Unfortunately, emergency treatment is sometimes required. Fortunately, Bermuda's health care system is ranked among the best. In an emergency, dial 911 from any telephone and an ambulance will soon be on the way. If you are ambulatory, you'll go to the King Edward VII Memorial Hospital, 7 Point Finger Road, Paget Parish, 441-236-2345.

If you require medical attention while in Bermuda, payment will be expected at the time of treatment. Unfortunately, they do not accept any foreign medical insurance.

Telephones

The area code for Bermuda is 441; the official website for the Bermuda Telephone Company is www.btc.bm.

Public telephones are strategically placed around the islands, and pre-paid calling cards can be purchased almost anywhere, even at dispensing machines. Local calls cost 40¢; just deposit four 10¢ coins and dial. If you don't have the necessary change, you can deposit a quarter, but the pay phones do not give change. Telco (441-295-1001) has its office at 30 Victoria Street and you can purchase pre-paid calling cards there, or at any one of a number outlying branches.

Bermuda also has an independent long-distance carrier, TeleBurmuda International (TBI), whose rates are generally cheaper than those of Telco. And a neat thing about TBI cards is that if you're from the US, Canada or the UK, you can use them when you get home. They can be pre-purchased in $10, $25 and $50 denominations, or from TBI's Customer Care Centre at 30 Victoria Street, Hamilton, 441-295-1001.

International Calls

As always, when in a foreign country, international calls made from a hotel can be extremely expensive. I've found one of the best strategies is to make prior arrangements with one of your home carriers, such as AT&T. Better yet, those computer outfits, such as Vonage or Magic Jack, will allow you to use your cell phone and you call for home for nothing. Arrange before you leave to have your foreign destination added to your long distance service at very competitive rates, and when you call home (home phone number only) using your AT&T calling card, you'll get the same low rate. For instance, a call from the US to Bermuda can be as low as 35¢ and the same rate will apply when you make a calling card call from Bermuda to your home phone number.

Be aware that some US carriers have no service from Bermuda, so check before you go. Some carriers also charge an international connection fee; be prepared for sticker shock. And check with your hotel to see if they impose any charges over and above those of your international carrier. Some do, and you might get an unexpected surprise when you receive your bill on check-out. Also find out what your hotel's policy is regarding local calls; some charge for these, too.

To call the US and Canada using a credit card or calling card, dial 0 plus the area code and number. Otherwise, dial 011 plus the area code and number.

Cell Phones

Yes, you can take your cell phone with you. Provided you have a compliant cell phone, that is. Cell phone use has gotten a lot easier over the last couple of years. Most manufacturers build GSM (Global System for Mobiles) technology into their equipment as a matter of course, especially in Europe. In the US, all one needs is the properly-equipped cell phone, a call to your provider and a request for the international dialing option, and you're ready to go. The international dialing option will cost you nothing: the roaming service, however, can be quite expensive – anywhere from $1 to $5 per minute.

If your phone is not "international capable," you can always rent one from your local provider before you leave. It's not cheap – usually $40 to $50 per week – and then you'll also have cough up for airtime, at least $1 per minute. Most of the national providers – Verizon, AT&T, etc. – offer cell phone rental by the week. Other options in the USA include Roadpost (888-290-1606) and InTouch USA, 800-872-7626).

In the US, if you'd like to find out if your cell phone will work in the Bermuda, call 800-872-7626 or go online to www.intouchglobal.com. Tell them where you're going and when, and they will give you rates. The good news is: if you happen to own a Sony Ericsson, Motorola or Samsung, your cell phone probably IS world-capable, but just to be sure check with your provider.

Much happier news for visitors from Europe: all of your providers use the GSM system, so you should be able to take your instruments with you. Better check on the rates, though. You might be in for a shock when you return home. For residents and long-term visitors, cellular service is readily available on the islands, but rather more expensive than you might be used to. At the time of writing, activation is just $10. However there's also a daily access charge of $5. Peak-time minutes (7 am-7 pm) cost 60¢; off-peak minutes, 35¢.

For cellular service while on the island, you'll need to contact BTC Mobility (Telco's cellular arm) about a week before you leave home. You can have your bill charged to Visa, MasterCard or American Express. If you're visiting Bermuda by private boat or yacht, call BTC for activation when you get within 50 miles of the islands. 441-292-6032, www.mobilityltd.bm/main.asp. Cell phones can be rented by the day in Bermuda for as little as $2 per day. The rates are quite competitive: day and night 'air time' use for local calls is 60 cents a minute and there's no charge for the extra services provided (call waiting, voice mail etc.).

Calls to the UK, USA, and Canada are an additional 50 cents a minute, i.e.: 110 cents a minute. International calls to the rest of the world are only one dollar per minute. Contact Robin Henagulph, P.O. Box 110, Devonshire DV BX, Bermuda or by phone 24 hours at 441-232-2355, fax 441-236-1827 or visit www.bermudacellrental.com.

Using the Internet

Most of Bermuda's major hotels offer high-speed internet access either via Ethernet cable or wireless connection. The cost runs from $12 to $20 per day, depending upon the hotel.

There are several internet cafes in Hamilton, including: Internet Lane, 22 Reid Street, Hamilton, 441-296-9972, info@internetlane.net, and www.internetlane.net. Internet Lane offers high speed internet access and is a state-of-the art facility where you can check your e-mail, chat to friends, surf the net and whatever else. There are computers for use by the Lane's patrons, or you can bring your own laptops.

Another opportunity is the Freeport Seafood Restaurant, Royal Naval Dockyard, Sandy's Parish, 441-234-1692. They, too, offer internet access through on-site computers for the use of their patrons, or you can bring your own laptop.

The IPass network offers dial-up service almost everywhere in Bermuda. It's a bit of a pain to use – you have to get them to help you set up your computer for Bermuda. To get a list of IPass providers, go online to www.ipass.com and then click on "Individuals." Select your country (Bermuda) and this is what you'll find: "Worldwide Dialup – We are the solution for individuals, small to medium size businesses and Universities! Worldwide Dialup provides an easy to use, fully supported IPass dialup and broadband service, with 24x7x365 support, email with Spam and Virus Filtering, on-line account administration and a fully redundant network. Our staff provides technical assistance regardless of your operating system - from Windows to Mac to Palm, we can even point you in the right direction if you are using other non-supported systems for connectivity (Linux, Unix, etc.). Our rates are extremely competitive!" They are out of Ada, Michigan and, yes, you'll have to call for current rates, 616-682-4813, fax 616-682-1389. In the end, though, I'm not sure it's entirely worth it, especially with almost all hotels on the island providing service of one sort or another, even if it's only via the hotel guest's business office.

Postal Service

Bermuda's post office is at 11 Queen Street in Hamilton. However, found all over the islands are red Royal Mail post boxes, called pillar-boxes (just like the ones in England) where you can deposit mail. Mail is collected from them daily. Letters and postcards take at least a week to reach the US or the UK, so be sure to mail your cards during the first day or two of your visit or else you may arrive home before they do.

Getting Around

Renting a car is not an option; there is no such service. Those over age 16 may rent a moped or a bicycle; a driver's license is not required. The only difficulty, depending on what part of the world you live in, is riding on the left side of the road!

Public Transportation

Public transportation in Bermuda is world-class. The pretty pink busses provide non-stop service to all parts of the island and, as they say, there really will be another one along in a minute. And the ferry service between Hamilton, the Royal Naval Dockyard, Paget - Warwick and St. George is the unique and enjoyable way to travel around the island.

Photo Courtesy of the Bermuda Department of Tourism

The Ferry System is Unique to Bermuda, and a terrific way to see the island from the water.

You'll find Bus Schedules and Ferry Information at the end of this book.

Private transportation in Bermuda is available in the form of taxis, scooter rentals, pedal cycles, the Bermuda Railways Train in Dockyard, Hamilton and St. George's;

as well as 19-foot whaler boat rentals for water exploration.

Note: the rates for bike and moped/scooter rentals listed below were correct at the time of writing. Like all things, however, rates are subject to change at a moment's notice. Be sure to shop around before you pay.

Bicycles are popular on the islands. They are cheap to rent, convenient, easy to park, and no destination is too far away. You'll find bikes to rent at most hotels and at the ubiquitous cycle shops. Touring the island by bicycle allows you to truly absorb the beauty that surrounds you. The Royal Naval Dockyard at the West End is less than two hours from Hamilton by bicycle. You can return by ferry if the ride back is more than you can handle. The daily rate for a bicycle is $55; it's cheaper by the week, 7 days costs $155.

Mopeds

Mopeds are the accepted for of travel in Bermuda, and they are an adventure all their own. Mopeds can be rented at many of the island hotels and resorts or at nearby cycle shops, where the rates are somewhat lower. The going rate for a moped runs from about $50 a day. Rates are much lower if you rent for several days – by the week (7 days) you can expect to pay around $220. Rates are all-inclusive, offering basic instruction, a tank of gas, helmets (required by law), a lock and key, insurance, breakdown service and even pick-up and delivery. You will be required to leave a small deposit, usually $30 to $50, to cover loss of the helmet, lock and key.

Gas stations are open from 7 am until 7 pm. Gas for mopeds costs around $2.88 per liter. Sound like a lot? Maybe, but a moped runs forever on a gallon.

Never ridden a moped before? Don't worry. It won't take more than a few minutes to learn, but even for experienced riders the adventure can be a little hazardous. The roads on Bermuda, while well-paved and without potholes, are always crowded, narrow and winding, with one blind curve after another.

The best way to avoid accidents is to stay strictly within the speed limit: a sedate 20 miles per hour. Once you've become used to riding on the left, you're in for a rare treat. The island roads will take you through a dozen communities with pastel-painted houses, well-kept colorful gardens, parks full of flowers and tiny churches. The coast roads offer magnificent views of the beaches (there's one at almost every turn), little country stores, national parks and the inviting turquoise ocean. There's no need to rush.

Some other things you should know when riding a bike or moped around Bermuda:

You must always give way to pedestrians on crosswalks. Zebra crossings have white stripes on the road and pelican crossings have pedestrian-operated red lights.

Wear appropriate clothing: bathing suits, bare feet and flip-flop sandals are not allowed on motorized cycles, and they're not a good idea even on a peddle cycle.

Bermuda law requires that you wear a helmet when riding a moped.

When approaching a roundabout – England's most notorious type of intersection – you must give way to traffic already on the roundabout approaching from the right; once you get onto the roundabout, you have right of way. Never stop on a roundabout.

The Tribe Roads

Tribe roads are quaint little lanes an alleyways that are just a delight to explore. Back in the 1600s, the parishes were known as tribes, hence the name "the tribe roads." Almost all tribe roads run north to south, with many of them meandering through parts of Bermuda's most desolate areas. Some are fairly well-used thoroughfares, some are little more than footpaths, and all make great walking trails. There was a time when there were more than 40 tribe roads; today there are about 30. Of those, I've been able to find only a half-dozen. Searching out the rest would be a fun and interesting exercise. The ideal way to do it would be to rent a bike or moped, pack a sack lunch from the hotel, and head out in the early morning along one of the major east/west highways, keeping a sharp lookout along the way for these ancient and secret roads. One of these days, I intend to do just that.

Bicycle & Moped Rental Companies

All rental companies listed below accept major credit cards, supply the necessary safety gear, and require that you leave a small refundable deposit against the loan of equipment.

Wheels Cycle, 441-292-224, has two locations on Front Street in Hamilton: one at Flatts Village and one at Grotto Bay Hotel.

Oleander Cycles Ltd., Valley Road, P.O. Box 114, Paget Parish, 441-236-5235 rents only scooters. $55 first day; extra days have price reductions depending on the length of rental. Insurance is $30. Oleander also has locations on Gorham Road in Hamilton, 441-295-0919, and at Middle Road in Southampton, 441-234-0629. The Paget and Southampton locations are open daily 8:30am to 5:30pm; the Hamilton branch is open daily 8:30am to 5pm.

Eve's Cycle Livery 441-236-6247, rents a variety of scooters; they cost from around $49 for the first day with lower prices for each additional day. You can also rent by the week - $210 to $249 for 7 days - depending on the model.

Smatt's Cycle Livery, Ltd., 74 Pitts Bay Rd., Hamilton, Pembroke Parish, 441-295-1180, is next door to the Fairmont Hamilton Princess Hotel. They have about 100 motorbikes on hand, priced from about $50 for a 1-day rental of a single-seater; $75 for a two-seater; rent by the week from $225. An insurance premium of $30 is added onto the rental price. Staff provides instruction on riding, safety and protocol.

Buses

I absolutely love traveling around the island on Bermuda's modern pink and white buses. They are comfortable, run frequently, go just about everywhere and are almost always on time. There's an old saying about the busses in London: "Don't worry, there'll be another one along in a minute; and that's exactly how it is in Bermuda. Better Yet, there's nowhere that more than a few hundred yards from the nearest bus stop.

Expect to pay, depending upon the zone, either $3 to $4.50 per ride. You can also purchase a daily pass for $12, two days for $20, and so on up to $45 for a 7-day pass. The more days you buy, the cheaper the rates. You can buy them either at the bus station or the Tourist Information Office at the Ferry Dock. The passes allow unlimited travel during the period of validity both on buses and ferries. They even include entry to the lighthouse on Gibbs Hill. The savings offered by these all-inclusive passes over a single ticket can be staggering. For more information visit www.bermudabuses.com.

Bus stops are marked by pink and blue poles. Poles with a pink section at the top indicate the stop is for inward-bound buses going to Hamilton; those with a blue section at the top are outward-bound from Hamilton.

To stop a bus you MUST stand by the pink and blue pole! Be on the lookout for fast-moving traffic.

For Lost & Found on Bermuda buses, 441-292-3851.

The Buses and Bus Schedules:

Bermuda has one of the easiest to use public bus services in the world. The system is divided in 14 fare zones of about 2 miles length and fares are based on the number of zones travelled. Buses require exact fare in local currency, tokens, or prepaid tickets; transfers are available. Single- or multiple-day transportation passes, accepted on buses and ferries, can be purchased. Children under age five ride free, and at age 5–15 pay a reduced rate.

Bus Schedules: If you have the correct time – watch, cell phone, whatever – you don't need to worry too much about the actual schedules - I never have - because no matter where you might be on the island, or at what time, so long as it's between 7 am and 11 pm, there's always a bus just around the corner, just a few minutes away. They run at variable (often 15-minute) intervals; so, as they say, there'll be another one along in just a minute. All you need do is find one of those pink (inbound towards Hamilton) or Blue (outbound from Hamilton) poles they are everywhere - then stand and wait. Buses stop at them on request. – You won't wait for long, I promise.

There are pink and blue bus stop poles on the roads at all of the major hotels, guest houses, resorts and cottage colonies

Most visitors from cruise ships use the bus system; however, airline passengers cannot transport luggage on the buses and generally prefer the taxi or airport limo system.

Bus Routes

All but one bus route start from the bus terminal in Hamilton.

Route 1 – Round trip from Hamilton to Grotto Bay and St. George's

Route 2 - Round trip from Hamilton to Ord Road

Route 3 - Round trip from Hamilton to Grotto Bay and St. George's

Route 4 - Round trip from Hamilton to Spanish Point

Route 5 - Round trip from Hamilton to Pond Hill

Route 6 - Round trip from St. George's to St. David's (it's the only way to get there, other than by taxi)

Route 7 - Round trip from Hamilton to Barnes Corner via the beaches on the South Shore Road (this really puts the beaches within easy reach, and quickly.

Route 8 & 8C - Round trip from Hamilton to Barnes Corner; Hamilton to the Dockyard; Hamilton to Somerset via Middle Road

Route 9 - Round trip from Hamilton to Prospect (National Stadium)

Route 10 - Round trip from Hamilton to St. George's via North Shore past Aquarium

Route 11 - Round trip from Hamilton to St. George's via North Shore Road

Bus Routes -Eastern Areas

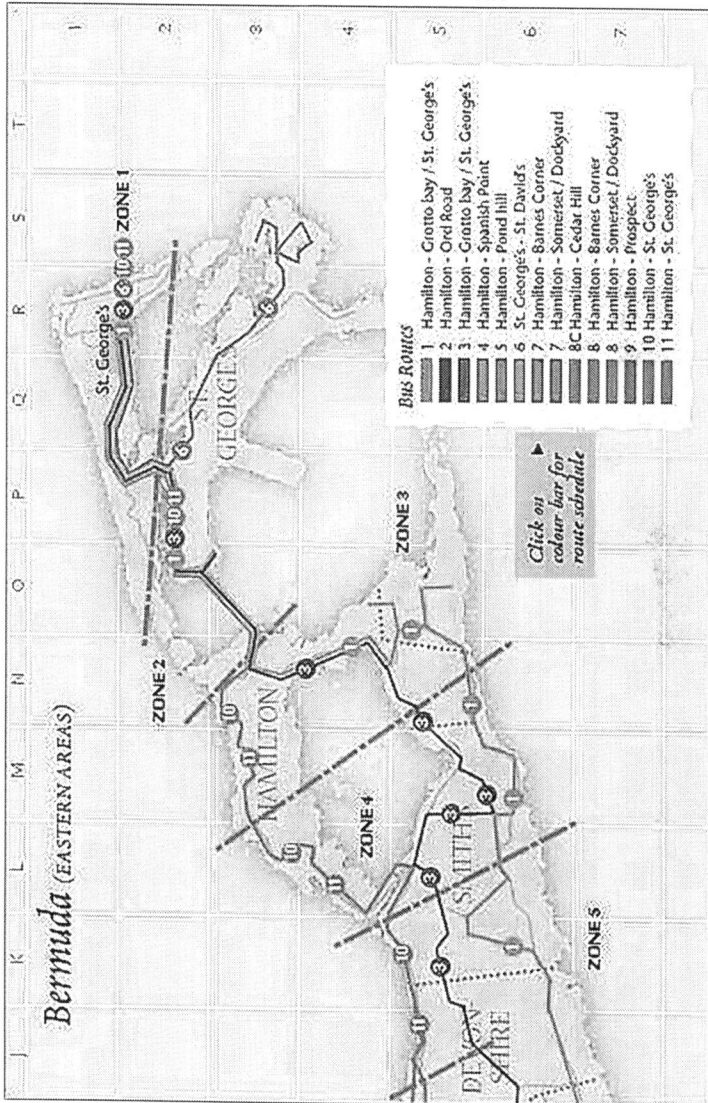

Bus Routes

1. Hamilton - Grotto bay / St. George's
2. Hamilton - Ord Road
3. Hamilton - Grotto bay / St. George's
4. Hamilton - Spanish Point
5. Hamilton - Pond hill
6. St. George's - St. Davids
7. Hamilton - Barnes Corner
7. Hamilton - Somerset / Dockyard
8C Hamilton - Cedar Hill
8. Hamilton - Barnes Corner
8. Hamilton - Somerset / Dockyard
9. Hamilton - Prospect
10 Hamilton - St. George's
11 Hamilton - St. George's

Click on colour bar for route schedule

Bermuda (EASTERN AREAS)

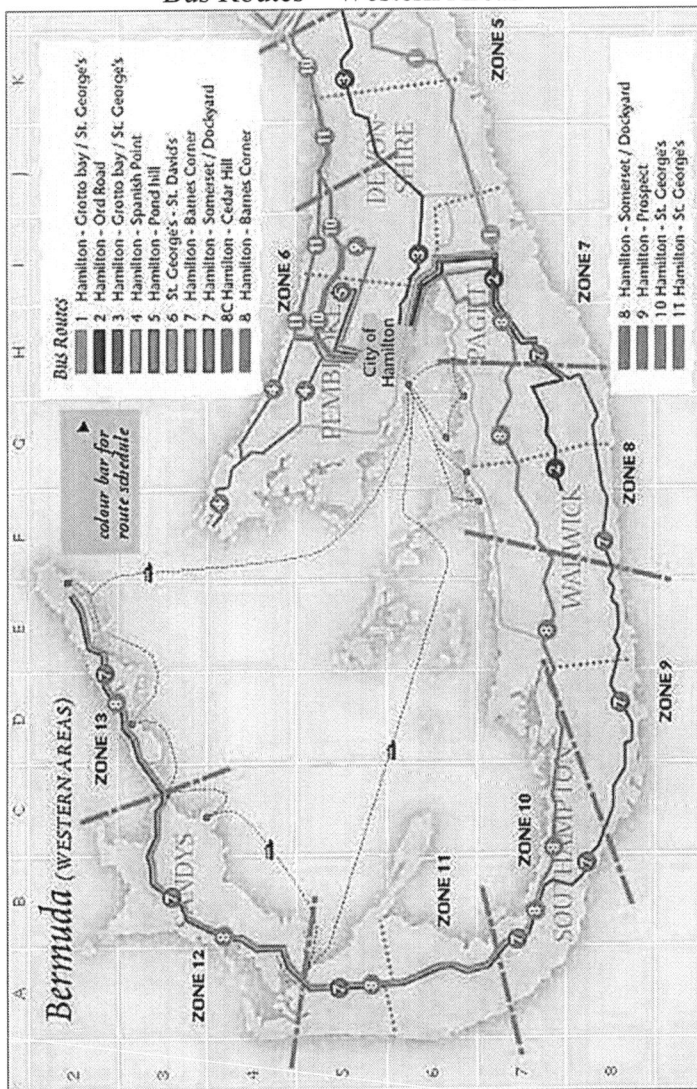

Ferries

The ferry system in Bermuda is, in my opinion, even better than the busses. A ferry ride is not just a way of getting from one place to another, it's an adventure, and a thoroughly enjoyable one. There's nothing quite like a boat ride on a warm, sunny day.

Photo Courtesy Captain Tucker & Creative Commons

Ferries boats run between Hamilton and Paget, Warwick, Somerset and the Royal Naval Dockyard. You can go out on the ferry and return by bus or vice-versa. The boat ride to the Dockyard takes about 30 minutes. A round-trip to the Dockyard, then along the coast to Grey's Bridge, Watford Bridge Wharf to Somerset and back to Hamilton, takes a good hour and can be a delightful experience.

The ferry boats plies back and forth between Paget and Hamilton every 30 minutes or so. The fare between Paget or Warwick and Hamilton is $4.50 each way for adults. If you are carrying a bicycle, it will cost an additional $4. The tickets (a book of 15 for $30) are valid for ferry rides as well. Bicycles and mopeds are not allowed on the smaller ferry boats between Warwick or Paget and Hamilton. The travel passes mentioned above really comes into its own when traveling by ferry.

Over the course of a week, you'll probably ride the ferry a number of times; with the average round-trip costing around $9, savings can be significant.

Yes, the ferry is the way to go. You can spend hours or days just riding back and forth or around the sound. The larger boats that travel the waters between Hamilton and Somerset have snack bars that sell hot dogs, muffins, sandwiches and ice-cold drinks. Sit inside and watch the world go by through the big windows or take a breath of fresh air on the observation deck and enjoy the sun and salt-spray tickling your face. Contact 441-295-4506 or www.seaexpress.bm for additional information.

Bermuda Ferry Information

On Saturdays the first ferry leaves Hamilton at 8:15 am and the last at 9:45 pm. Sundays & holidays, the first ferry leaves at 10:10, the last at 7 pm. Note that bikes are not allowed on the Pink Route.

Blue Route – Monday to Friday (Hamilton - West End - Dockyard)
Blue Route – Saturday (Hamilton - West End - Dockyard)
Pink Route (Hamilton - Paget - Warwick)
Orange Route (Hamilton - Dockyard - St. George's)
Green Route – Monday to Friday (Hamilton – Rockaway Express)

Store Hours

Hours for most stores are from 9 am until 5 pm, Monday through Saturday. But you will find some stores are now staying open later, especially on and around Front Street in Hamilton. With the exception of the stores at the Royal Naval Dockyard at the West End, all shops are closed on Sunday and legal holidays. Restaurants open at 11 am on weekdays and at noon on Saturday.

Photo Courtesy of the Bermuda Department of Tourism

Sightseeing

The Beaches

Nowhere on earth are there more beautiful per capita than in Bermuda. This tiny island boasts of 34 of the most beautiful beaches in the world. The sand has a pink tinge to it (best seen when wet), caused by particles of sea shells mixed with native coral and calcium carbonate.

The heart of the Bermudian public beach system is the South Shore National Park, which covers 1½ miles of coastline. The park has more than 11 beaches that extend from Port Royal Cove to the eastern end of Warwick Long Bay. These beaches vary considerably in size and nature. Some, like the half-mile-long Warwick Long Bay, are unbroken expanses; others are tiny secluded coves separated from one another by rocky cliffs. Port Royal Cove, Peel Bay, Jobson's Cove and Horseshoe Bay offer tiny private beaches and sheltered natural pools.

The South Shore itself, with its crystal-clear water to the front and miles of nature trails behind, is a good place to sunbathe, walk, swim, snorkel or jog. It glimmers in the early morning light and glows under a spectacular evening sunset. On a cloudy day during the winter, the character of the South Shore changes to one of splendid isolation. The air is crisp and refreshing, brisk breezes blow salt spray high into the air, and the ocean is bracing.

Along the shoreline you'll see low outcrops of rock, roughly circular in shape. Created by constant wave action that hollows out the soft inner rock, these outcrops are commonly known as reefs or boilers. The scientific name for these anomalies is algal-vermetid reefs, or serpuline atolls. On calm days, the waters around the boilers are great for snorkeling as dozens of gaily colored fish come here in search of shelter and food. You might spot an angelfish, parrotfish, trumpet fish or even a grouper.

Starting at the west end of the island and working eastward along the South Shore, the following descriptions will give you an idea of what to expect at each beach or park.

A Word of Warning: Snorkeling, swimming and wading are everyday activities at all of the popular beaches around Bermuda, and these activities are, for the most part, very safe. There are, however, a couple of things that you should be on the lookout for. Coral is sharp and will cut unprotected feet and hands, and any other exposed part of the body. A coral wound can be extremely painful and can lead to infection if left uncared for. Always wear shoes; better yet, stay away from coral heads altogether (coral is an endangered species). The other thing to be on the lookout for is the Portuguese man-o'war – a jellyfish. They are prevalent around the islands from March through July and are often very big. Their tentacles can trail more than 50 feet from the brilliant blue balloon that acts as a sail and propels it through the water.

Sandy's Parish

Parson's Bay (Lagoon Park, Lagoon Road)

A sheltered area of beach popular with the locals as a picnic spot. It's not near a bus stop, so you'll need to get there on your bike or moped. You'll find it on Lagoon Road just before it becomes Craddock Road. The strip has white sand and the area is usually quiet.

Mangrove Bay (Mangrove Bay Road)

Just a short distance from the shopping area in Somerset Village. It's a favorite with the locals, but is usually quiet enough during the week for a picnic, some sun and a swim. The swimming is considered safe, but it's always best to keep an eye on the young kids. It's a picturesque strip with mangroves that line the beach and follow the gentle curve of the shoreline.

Somerset Long Bay Park Beach (Daniel's Head)

Reminiscent of the traditional English village green, Somerset Long Bay Park is where the locals of Somerset Village take time out on weekends for a picnic and the eternal English game of cricket. Then there's the beach, also popular as a picnic spot, with its long, sweeping shoreline, white sand and shallow waters. The swimming here is safe for kids – at low tide the water is rarely deep enough to give concern. During the week, you can count on having most of the beach to yourself. Long walks, hot sun, snorkeling and lazy days make this the ideal spot to get away from it all. Restrooms are available in the park. Somerset Long Bay Park is one of the nicest public parks on the islands.

Southampton Parish

Church Bay Beach (Church Bay Park, South Road)

The reef and the potboilers (isolated rocks sticking up out of the surf) at Church Bay Beach are close to shore, so is one for the snorkelers. Just an easy swim and you're in the middle of more marine life than you ever imagined. Easy to recognize is the rock protruding from the ocean known to the locals as Poodle Rock. From a certain angle it does look exactly like a poodle. The sandy beach is a nice place to hang out, but is only incidental to the underwater delights just offshore. Where the sand meets the sea it quickly gives way to a rocky bottom.

Slip on your flippers and mask and head out to the rocks. You can expect to see all sorts of finny inhabitants of the reef, along with some hard-shell ones as well. Look for butterfly fish, angels and parrotfish, to name but a few. Done swimming? Take a few moments to enjoy the park. There's a ruined fort on the cliff near the parking lot, some picnic tables where you can enjoy a quiet lunch, and public restrooms.

Warning: The water gets deep very quickly at Church Bay Beach and is often quite rough, so it's not the place to let the kids loose without close supervision.

Horseshoe Bay (South Shore Park off South Road)

Horseshoe Bay is, without doubt, the most popular beach/park on the islands, and the most famous. Don't expect a quiet afternoon in the sun here. Even on weekdays you'll find it crowded; on weekends it can be overwhelming. But there's good reason: it's one of the most picturesque spots on the islands and the most photographed. I myself have snapped it from all angles and at all times of day, from early morning to early evening, and something new always seems to show up in the pictures. Horseshoe Bay is the first of a long line of beaches that stretches eastward for more than four miles. Yes, you can make the walk if you're the energetic type.

The Rocks at Horseshoe Bay
Photo Courtesy of the Bermuda Department of Tourism

If you're visiting by cruise ship, and you're short on time, you must try and make it to Horseshoe Bay; it's a must-see for anyone visiting Bermuda for the first time. It's on the bus route (they run every 20 minutes or so). Ask the driver to stop at Horseshoe Bay. Leave the bus stop and make your way down the driveway into the park. Once there, you'll see the beach stretching away for about a quarter-mile. The ends are enclosed by high limestone cliffs, the sand is a pale pink, and the water is clear and blue. Early morning is the best time to visit: it's less crowded then, and you can walk the sandy stretches uninterrupted by crowds of sunbathers.

If you snorkeler. You'll find the waters just offshore among the rocks to be the best anywhere, but you'll need to be a strong swimmer; the swells are quite strong. Under the waves expect to see all sorts of colorful life, such as parrotfish, wrasse, angels, sergeant majors, snapper and many others. While at the beach, take time out for a light refreshment at the Horseshoe Bay Beach House, 441-238-2651. They serve great sandwiches and long, cool, drinks. Restrooms are available and the park is wheelchair-accessible.

Port Royal Cove (South Shore Park off South Road)

One of the smaller beaches along the South Shore, hence its nickname of Baby Beach, Port Royal Cove is extremely popular with both the locals and visitors. There's a nice, but somewhat small, sandy beach (it can be quite crowded at times) and a deep-water pool where you can leap from the rocks. The surrounding waters and rocky outcrops are ideal for snorkeling although the waters can get quite choppy at times. The sand is fine and pink, as is most of the sand along the South Shore; the waters are crystal clear, and the scenery surrounding the little beach is a photographer's dream. If you have small children with you, this is the ideal spot to bring them.

Warwick Parish

Chaplin's Bay (South Shore Park, South Road)

Chaplin's Bay is another of those little coves or bays, partially in Southampton Parish and partially in Warwick, one of those picturesque little spots that makes this area so pleasant and appealing. It's also a popular spot, and is often too busy for those who like to get away from it all. But, if you get there in the early morning, you're likely to have it all to yourself.

Jobson's Cove (South Shore Park, South Road)

Jobson's Cove is one of the most popular spots on the South Shore. You're sure to enjoy a visit to Jobson's. It's rather tiny as beaches go – just a few square yards, in fact – but visually it's spectacular. This is another ideal spot to take the kids, for the tiny cove is completely surrounded by rocks, making the shallow waters unusually calm most of the time. The sand is fine and pink, and the beach is sheltered from even the strongest breezes. It's a great spot for a picnic. At least it would be if it weren't quite so busy. Get there early and pick your spot.

Jobson's Cove
Photo Courtesy of the Bermuda Department of Tourism

Warwick Long Bay (South Shore Park, South Road)

Warwick Long Bay is... well..."Long." In fact, it stretches almost the entire length of the South Shore Park, for as far as you can see eastward. Warwick Long Bay is a vast stretch of pink sand that curves gently away into the distance. There's room enough for everyone here – more sea and sand than you can imagine – so it's rarely crowded, even on weekends.

Photo Courtesy of the Bermuda Department of Tourism

Warning: Warwick Long Bay is not the ideal beach to turn the kids loose. You'll need to keep an eye on them constantly, and you shouldn't let them venture into the water on their own. The sea can turn quite rough and the sandy bottom is apt to drop off quite suddenly. Undercurrents can also be a problem.

Warwick Long Bay is a great place to spend the day, with or without kids. The South Shore Park, with its public services, runs almost the entire length of the bay. Hours can be spent wandering the shoreline and the park itself has cliffs, woodland trails and delightful landscaping. There's also a playground for the kids with swings, slides and ropes; all good fun. Time for something to eat? Take advantage of the concession stand just across the road above the beach for sandwiches and ice cream.

Astwood Cove (Astwood Park, South Road)

Astwood Cove is situated at the eastern end of Warwick Long Bay. If you like to do a little bird watching, this is the place for you. There are more open spaces in this park, which makes it somewhat different from South Shore Park, and it's usually quiet. Narrow footpaths meander along the cliff-tops, through fields and dunes; it's a place where you can get close to nature. The beach itself is inviting with fine sand and crystal waters, which can become little rough at times, but are ideal for snorkeling, especially among the rocks just offshore.

Warning: While it's a great place for the more adventurous older kids, you'll need to keep an eye on the littler ones, and stay with them when they venture into the water.

Paget Parish

Elbow Beach (Tribe Road #4, South Road)

This magnificent stretch of pink sand is the jewel in Paget's crown. Unfortunately, it's only partially open to the public; the eastern section is the private domain of the Elbow Beach Hotel and can be accessed only through the hotel grounds. The western section of the beach, however, is one of the best beaches on the islands (at least in my opinion).

Take the bus or a scooter along South Road to Tribe Road #4. From there it's but a short walk along the Tribe Road to the beach. There you'll find changing facilities, beach chairs and a couple of nice cafés/restaurants where you can enjoy lunch or dinner. The $5 fee (payable as you enter the beach) entitles you to the use of all the facilities. The beach itself is a world of dunes and shore where you can relax, swim and sunbathe to your heart's content. The water is clear and inviting, ideal for a family outing, but you do need to keep an eye on the younger members; don't let them play in the water unattended.

Pembroke Parish.

Clarence Cove (Spanish Point)

Spanish Point is on the North Shore and you get there from Hamilton either by bus or on foot. If you decide to walk, it's an easy hike of about two miles.

If you have small children, you'd better to take the bus either from the terminal on Washington Street or from the bus stop in front of the Tourist Information Center on Front Street.

Spanish Point was named for a Spanish sea captain whose ship was wrecked on the rocks just off the point. Admiralty House Park was named for the building in the park that once did service to the lords of the Royal Navy. Today the house is a community center. Two small beaches inside the park are reached via a footpath that leads downhill to the shore.

These secluded little sandy places are considered safe for all members of the family, including small children. Most of the time, perhaps due to their location, they are quiet, without the bustling crowds sometimes the bane of the beaches on the South Shore. Only during July and August when they are the venue for summer camps do they get busy – it's then that you might consider visiting a less-crowded beach.

Smith's Parish

John Smith's Bay Park and Beach (South Road)

John Smith's Bay Park and Beach is yet another South Shore local favorite, so it can get extremely busy, especially on weekends. The wide, sandy beach and clear shallow waters make it safe for small children and, offshore, deeper waters and a reef that makes it a snorkeler's dream. Hundreds of colorful reef fish such as sergeant majors, parrotfish, jacks, blue and yellow grunts, angels, butterfly fish and wrasse casually swim by.

John Smith's Bay Beach
Photo Courtesy of the Bermuda Department of Tourism

At times, you'll see warning flags at the beach lifeguard station indicating that water conditions may be dangerous. Check with a lifeguard (on duty during summer) before venturing into deep waters.

The park offers public toilets/restrooms, but there are no other conveniences close by. During the summer a mobile concession stand visits the park to sell soft drinks, coffee, tea and sandwiches (they're good!).

Hamilton Parish

Shelly Bay Beach (South Road)

Back on the South Shore, in Hamilton Parish, is where you'll find Shelly Bay Park, a great place to spend a day. A beach house sells snacks, soft drinks and ice cream, and there are bathrooms, changing rooms and rental lockers for stowing away those odds and ends that always seem to get lost in the sand. Rent snorkeling equipment here ($5/hour and up), towels ($2.50/day and up), loungers ($12/day and up) and umbrellas ($2.50/day and up). Like to go sailing? Try a Hobe Cat ($50/per hour) or something slower like a peddle boat ($25/first hour, $10/each additional hour). The beach offers lots of clean sand (though somewhat gritty) and crystal-clear waters shallow enough for small children. A playground in the park has swings, slides and climbing frames galore – enough to keep even the most active kids happy for an hour or two.

St. George's Parish

Tobacco Bay Park (Coot Pond Road)

Tobacco Bay Beach
Photo Courtesy of the Bermuda Department of Tourism

Also available are fast food and soft drinks, changing rooms and bathrooms. The beach itself, although small and sometimes crowded, is considered safe for all members of the family and has lots of shallow water. Offshore, the rocks make for great snorkeling: plenty of color and life in the form of sergeant majors, parrotfish, jacks, blue and yellow grunts, angels, butterfly fish and wrasse.

Another popular spot with locals, Tobacco Bay Beach, on Coot Pond Road, has a Pavilion (right on the beach), where you can rent all sorts of equipment and conveniences such as loungers ($2/ hour), beach umbrellas ($5/day) and snorkeling gear ($12/two hours).

Other Beaches

There several other beaches that are also worth a mention:

St. Catherine's Beach on the eastern shore of St. George's; Clearwater Beach on Mercury Road (also in St. George's); and Coral Beach and Marley Beach on the South Shore, both located between Astwood Park and Elbow Beach.

Lifeguards & Warning Flags

During the summer months (June through October) you'll find lifeguards on duty at many public beaches from 10 am until 6 pm. A white flag at the lifeguard tower indicates an on-duty lifeguard. Also, warning flags tell beachgoers of any possible swimming hazards: a yellow flag warns that water conditions are questionable (consult a lifeguard before entering the water); a red flag means that conditions are unsafe for swimming – take heed and stay out of the water.

Hiking:

Bermuda is a hiker's paradise. Almost all of the island can easily be explored on foot, so there's little point in going into depth about the tribe roads, parks, and such, with the exception of the Railway Trail, a unique and not-to-be-missed hiking experience.

There's virtually nowhere on the islands that you can't walk. Most people take to the main roads – watch out for the traffic – and, of course, there are a great number of beaches and parks that are open to the public. In addition, many of the Tribe Roads provide access to parts of Bermuda that are rarely seen by the visitor, and the Railway Trail offers a special hiking experience that will take you from one end of the island to the other. For detailed walks and tours, see Touring the Parishes.

Be sure to wear reflective gear if you intend to walk after dark. The main roads are often narrow and include many quick, blind curves.

The Bermuda Railway Trail

Perhaps the most exciting and diverse hiking experience here is the Bermuda Railway Trail, where some of the loveliest sightseeing can be enjoyed from any number of natural vantage points. The old passenger railway offers stunning seascapes, breathtaking scenery, exotic plant and wildlife, apart from the busy roads and streets that have become the Bermuda of today.

Bermuda Railway Trail
Photo Courtesy of the Bermuda Department of Tourism

History

The Bermuda Railway was established in 1931 and the track stretched 21 miles around the island, crossing water and gorges via a series of 33 trestles and bridges. It was designed to transport people around Bermuda with ease and in relative comfort.

For many years it served its purpose well. The first-class section was furnished in old Colonial style, with wicker chairs, while the second class had wooden benches. The advent of the Second World War saw the beginning of the end for the old "Rattle and Shake."

By the end of the war the train was in poor shape. Faced with a repair bill in excess of a million dollars – quite a sum in those days – the Government of Bermuda decided to cut its losses and get rid of the old institution. They sold the system, lock stock and barrel, to British Guiana and, with the motor car receiving approval on the island in 1946, it was hardly missed at all.

During its 17 years of operation, the Bermuda Railway suffered not a single fatal accident and carried more than four million passengers. When the railway left Bermuda, all that remained was 21 miles of scenic right of way and a deep feeling of nostalgia among the islanders. For 30 years the old railway track remained unused. Now it's been turned into an unofficial national park where locals and visitors alike can enjoy the rails from one end of the islands to the other.

The Bermuda Railway Hiking Trail

The Bermuda Railway Trail incorporates almost the entire length of what once was Bermuda's passenger railway system. For than 20 miles, almost the entire length of the island, it meanders from east to west, or the other way around, should you so desire. The tracks and ties are long gone, but the way remains for all to enjoy. The trail is divided into seven geographical areas from east to west (see the map below) and, depending upon your location, you can walk from one end to the other, or you can hike it section by section.

The trail is accessible to hikers, joggers, bicyclists and walkers via 35 different access points. The sections vary in length from two to four miles, and each will take from two to four hours to complete. The Bermuda Railway trail is a serene world of stunning seascapes, breathtaking scenery, exotic plant and wildlife, apart from the sections that take in some of the busy roads and streets that have become the Bermuda of today.

If you're a serious hiker, you should first visit the Visitors Information Center on the ferry dock at Front Street in Hamilton and pick up a copy of The Bermuda Railway Trail Guide, a free pocket-size booklet that offers an interesting account of the railway's history and a detailed breakdown of the trail, section by section, with all the interesting sights along the way.

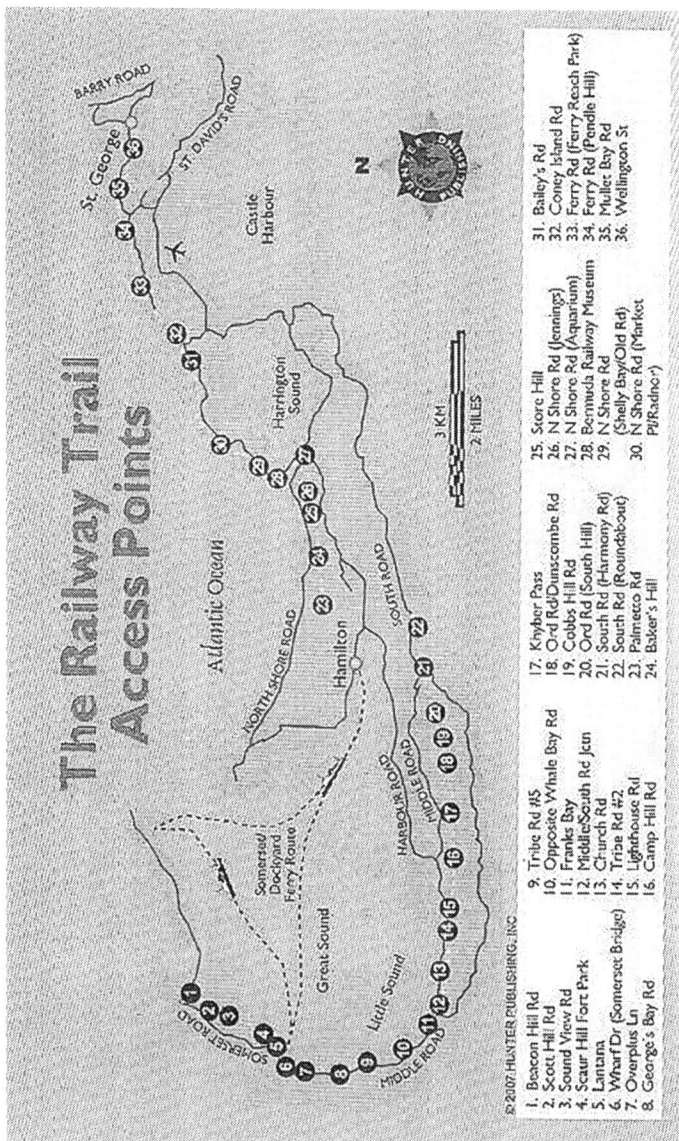

The Railway Trail Access Points

1. Beacon Hill Rd
2. Scott Hill Rd
3. Sound View Park
4. Scaur Hill Fort Park
5. Lantana
6. Wharf Dr (Somerset Bridge)
7. Overplus Ln
8. George's Bay Rd
9. Tribe Rd #5
10. Opposite Whale Bay Rd
11. Franks Bay
12. Middle/South Rd Jctn
13. Church Rd
14. Tribe Rd #2
15. Lighthouse Rd
16. Camp Hill Rd
17. Khyber Pass
18. Ord Rd/Dunscombe Rd
19. Cobbs Hill Rd
20. Ord Rd (South Hill)
21. South Rd (Harmony Rd)
22. South Rd (Roundabout)
23. Palmetto Rd
24. Baker's Hill
25. Store Hill
26. N Shore Rd (Jennings)
27. N Shore Rd (Aquarium)
28. Bermuda Railway Museum
29. N Shore Rd (Shelly Bay/Old Rd)
30. N Shore Rd (Market Pl/Radnor)
31. Bailey's Rd
32. Coney Island Rd
33. Ferry Rd (Ferry Reach Park)
34. Ferry Rd (Pendle Hill)
35. Muller Bay Rd
36. Wellington St

© 2007 HUNTER PUBLISHING, INC.

Map Courtesy of the Bermuda Department of Tourism

Touring the Parishes

Touring Pembroke Parish

Pembroke Parish, although some Bermudians might argue, is the heart of the islands. On the southern bank of Pembroke Parish is Bermuda's capital city of Hamilton. Everything seems to begin and end here. The government of the colony is based in the heart of the city. Buses begin and end their routes at the main terminal on Washington Street. Ferries cast off for ports on Great Sound from the dock at Front Street. And most of the fancy shops are in Hamilton.

The Bermuda Department of Tourism, 441-292-0023, is in Global House on Church Street. The staff is extremely helpful and will provide you with lots of informative material, including maps and brochures. The Visitors Service Bureau, 441-295-1480, is on Front Street at the entrance to the ferry terminal. Here, too, the staff is helpful, knowledgeable and can give suggestions for making the best of your vacation.

Touring the City of Hamilton

The City of Hamilton is the nerve center of Pembroke Parish and, of course, the island. It's the only city, by definition, on the islands (under British law, a city must have a cathedral; if not, it's a town or village). Hamilton was founded in 1790 and was named for Henry Hamilton, a one-time Royal Governor of the colony. Bermuda's capital was moved from St. George's to Hamilton in 1815. Its main thoroughfare, Front Street, presents a facade of pastel-painted buildings to the cruise ships that arrive weekly at **Hamilton Harbour**.

Today, the three-masted British naval ships and fast sailing clippers have been replaced by giant, modern cruise ships, seagoing freighters, pleasure craft of every shape and size, and public ferries. Passengers disembark directly onto Front Street, where they browse what once was known as the "Shop Window" of the British Empire. Even though the last vestiges of the British Naval presence left Bermuda in 1995, the area remains intact. Enjoy a pleasant walk along the seafront past dozens of colorful shop windows.

Front Street Shops – City of Hamilton
Photo Courtesy of the Bermuda Department of Tourism

To the west, at the junction of Front and Queen Streets, one of the few remaining police-operated traffic islands in the Caribbean (there's another in Nassau, Bahamas) is located in the center of the road. Inside the painted "**bird cage**," a Bermudian police officer – immaculately dressed in Bermuda shorts, crisp white shirt and traditional English bobby's helmet – directs traffic with an infectious enthusiasm. It's no wonder that they're the most photographed people on the island! If you plan to travel around the island by bus, you'll be making a number of visits to the bus terminal on Washington Street, 441-292-3854. Here you can purchase three- or seven-day travel passes.

From Front Street, take a walk north on Queen Street, turn right onto Church Street and cross the road in front of City Hall; the **bus station** is next to City Hall on the left. You'll see the rows of pink and blue buses. At the top of the hill on Church Street is Hamilton's magnificent **Anglican Cathedral of the Most Holy Trinity**, a superb example of Gothic architecture. Completed in 1991, the cathedral can accommodate a congregation of 1,000. The magnificent alter screen depicts all the saints for whom the island's parish churches are named, such as St. Andrew, St. George and St. Paul. Services are held every day and visitors are welcome. The Cathedral's tower looms 140 feet above this pastel-colored city. In the evening, the entire city becomes a fairyland of lighted buildings, capped by the cathedral. Hours: weekdays 10 am-3 pm. For services, 441-292-4033. Free admission to the Cathedral, admission to the tower is $3 for adults and $2 for children under seven and 65 and over.

Government House, the official residence of His Excellency, The Governor of Bermuda, stands high on Langton Hill overlooking Hamilton. The immaculate grounds of the house cover more than 45 acres. Unfortunately, the House is not open to the public.

In the open country just east of the city, **Fort Hamilton** stands among beautifully landscaped gardens and offers spectacular views of Hamilton, the harbor and the sound. Go east, either on Front Street or Reid Street, turn left onto King Street and then turn right on Happy Valley Road. The fort is on your left. It's quite a walk, but a pleasant one and well worth the effort as you step back in time to the 1860s. Built upon the orders of the Duke of Wellington, Fort Hamilton was obsolete before it was completed.

The passageways beneath the fort were hewn from the solid rock by soldiers of the British Corps of Engineers. The seacoast guns that stand guard over Hamilton and the harbor never fired a shot in anger.

A stirring event held at the fort every Monday at noon, March through November, features the Bermuda Pipe Band, complete with drummers and dancers, all wearing kilts.

Watch parliamentary debates at the **Sessions House** just a block east of the cathedral on Parliament Street. It's recognizable by its singular Victoria Jubilee Clock Tower, an outstanding example of Italian-style architecture. Hours: 9:30 am-12:30 pm, 2-5 pm weekdays.

The Bermuda House of Assembly, 441-292-7408, meets on the second floor and is in every way the British establishment it is meant to be. Proceedings are conducted with all the pomp and ceremony of the House of Commons in London. The Sergeant-at-Arms, bearing the Great Mace, precedes the Speaker of the House into the chamber. The Speaker then calls the house to order by banging an ancient gavel. View the proceedings from the public gallery.

Perhaps an even more enjoyable spectacle is the **Supreme Court**, 441-292-1350, on the lower floor of the Sessions House. Bewigged and be-cloaked barristers argue their cases before a panel of judges dressed in long, white wigs and bright red robes. The "Yes, me Luds," "No, me Luds," and "m'learned friends" fly around the room and provide great enjoyment to spectators. Call ahead to find out when they're in session.

Also on Church Street, a little farther west and opposite Queen Street, sits **City Hall**, a magnificent white building modeled after Stockholm's city hall. It houses a number of attractions, including the **Bermuda National Gallery** and a theater. To the rear of City Hall on Victoria Street is **Victoria Park**. It has lovely gardens and a Victorian bandstand, where concerts are held during the summer. The park, dedicated to Queen Victoria's Golden Jubilee, was opened in 1890. Unfortunately, it has become a gathering place for the low-life of the city; thus, it's not unusual to be accosted by beggars and other such undesirables here. Stay away from the park altogether after dark.

Opposite City Hall on Church Street is the entrance to the **Washington Mall**, a large two-story shopping center that stretches the entire block from Church to Reid Street. It hosts a diversity of stores, cafés and quaint little hole-in-the-wall shops - places where you can have a cup of hot tea and a sweet roll or find unique gifts for everyone at home.

Reid Street parallels Front Street just a block away to the south. It's the second busiest shopping area in Bermuda. Just across from the Washington Mall is the Walker Arcade.

Turn east, walk a short distance, and you'll find **Fagan's Alley**, another neat shopping center that runs from Reid Street all the way to Front Street. Turn west on Reid Street and you'll be back on Queen Street once more with the **Bermuda Public Library, the Historical Society Museum, the Perot Post Office, the Par-la-Ville Gardens**, and, just a short walk away on Front Street to the south, the bird cage traffic island. Before you leave Reid Street, however, be sure to stop at the Fourways Pastry Shop at the entrance to the Washington Mall. The pastries are a gourmet delight; bang goes the old diet, but never mind, you're on vacation!

Head south on Queen Street from Reid Street and you'll come to the **Perot Post Office**, 441-292-0952, a white two-story building on the right. It was here that the island's first postmaster set up shop in 1818. As it's been told, William Bennet Perot met arriving ships in the harbor, collected their mail and carried it around Hamilton inside his hat for delivery. It was Perot who introduced Bermuda's first stamp in 1848, although his motives, so it seems, were entirely selfish.

Postmaster by trade and gardener by choice, Perot begrudged the time he spent hand-stamping outgoing mail. His friend, J.B. Heyl, came up with a solution. He suggested that Perot hand-stamp a whole sheet of postmarks, sign each stamp, and sell the sheet for a shilling. People could tear off a stamp, glue it to the letter and mail it, all without Perot, who was now free to pursue his gardening. His stamps? Oh boy. They are extremely rare, each worth a half-million dollars or more.

The **Par-la-Ville Gardens**, next door to the Perot Post Office, now occupy almost an entire city block from Queen Street to Par-la-Ville Road and are a favorite lunch spot for local businesspeople. The gardens are beautifully landscaped with lots of flowers and shrubs and a network of paths. Benches make ideal picnic spots to eat those sumptuous pastries you bought at the **Fourways Pastry Shop**.

In front of the Par-la-Ville Gardens on Queen Street is a two-story house with a balcony. The house, set back a little from the street, was the home of the Perot family. Today it houses the **Bermuda Public Library** and the **Bermuda Historical Society Museum**, 441-292-0952. The old house is an adventure in its own right and has a number of collections, memorabilia and artifacts. The public library, founded in 1839, moved here in 1916. Its reference section has copies of Bermudian newspapers dating back to 1784 on microfilm. Among its collection of rare books is a 1624 edition of John Smith's General Historie of Virginia, New England and the Somer Isles.

Along with portraits of William Perot and his wife, you'll see magnificent portraits of Sir John Somers and his wife, which are thought to have been painted around 1605. There's also a map of Bermuda, dated 1624, that shows the division of the islands by the Bermuda Company into 25-acre shares. Other interesting exhibits include a collection of rare old English coins, furniture, fine china, a Waterford chandelier, handmade hats, clocks, and a collection of Confederate money that dates to the days of the blockade runners who ran from Bermuda into the southern ports of Charleston and Savannah. There is also a piece of lodestone that Sir George Somers used to magnetize his compass needles.

Even more interesting is a letter from **George Washington**, written in 1775, requesting supplies of gunpowder. You'll have to request a viewing if you'd like to see it. Hours: 9:30 am-3:30 pm, Monday-Saturday. Free.

While on Queen Street, you should visit the **Bermuda Book Store**. It stands right on the corner of Front and Queen and is a quaint old place, one you might more likely find on a back street in London than on the corner of the two busiest streets of a tropical island. Space inside the store is limited, with books of every size, color and topic crammed on its shelves. A narrow staircase takes you up to more books. The wood floorboards creak as you walk around, rather like an old library. If you'd like a book about the islands of Bermuda, this is the place to find it.

From Queen Street, turn right onto Front Street, go a short way to Point Pleasant Road, and you'll see the **Bank of Bermuda** in front of you. It houses one of the finest collections of British and Spanish coins outside Europe. The coins are exhibited in glass cases and include some fine examples of "hog money," Bermuda's first official currency, introduced by the Bermuda Company in 1616. When Sir George Somers and his companions were wrecked on the islands, the only inhabitants they found were wild hogs. It seemed only fitting that the first coins should depict a wild hog and the words "Somer Ilands" (the original spelling) on one side and the image of the Sea Venture on the other. Hog money is the oldest British colonial coinage. Hours: Monday, 9:30 am – 4 pm; Tuesday – Friday 8:30 am – 4:30 pm.

Just across the road from the Bank of Bermuda is the waterfront. **The Royal Bermuda Yacht Club**, established and given a Royal Charter in 1845, is just west of Point Pleasant Park. The Yacht Club is the hub of the Bermudian upper class. Here the elite of the islands mingles with the elite of the yachting world, international celebrities and even visiting royalty. The highlight of the Bermudian yachting calendar is, of course, the Newport to Bermuda Yacht Race.

Point Pleasant Park lives up to its name. It is, indeed, a pleasant spot to watch boats move in and out of the harbor. **Barr's Bay Park**, just west of the Yacht Club, also offers grand views of the sound and a quiet place to sit.

An agreeable walk of a couple of miles along Pitts Bay Road (the western extension of Front Street) will take you past the headquarters of the Bacardi Rum Company to the park at **Spanish Point**.

Too far to walk? Jump on a bus outside the Tourist Information Center on Front Street or at the terminal on Washington Street and ride out to the park in comfort.

The park is named for a Spanish captain whose ship ran aground on the rocks off the point. With the welfare of others in mind, he erected a wooden cross with written instructions outlining where nearby drinking water could be found. His directions were misunderstood, however, as a route to buried treasure, and later English settlers later searched and dug up the entire point to no avail. Today, the area affords inspiring views across Great Sound to Somerset and the Royal Naval Dockyard. It's a good place to sit and enjoy an afternoon in the sunshine or to go swimming and snorkeling off the wide, sandy beach.

Bermuda Underwater Exploration Institute & Ocean Discovery Centre, 40 Crow Lane, Hamilton, 441-297-7314, www.buei.org. The institute opened in 1997 to give the public an opportunity to explore the oceans around Bermuda to a depth of 12,000 feet. It's one of the most comprehensive and exciting exhibits of its type anywhere. The highlight is a simulated, seven minute "dive" to the ocean depths, taking the plunge with all the sights and sounds you'd experience if it were the real thing. Although seen through video screens instead of windows, the creatures you'll encounter on the journey downward seem real.

The Bermuda Underwater Exploration Institute
Photo Courtesy of the Bermuda Department of Tourism

Besides the dive, there are lots more exhibits to explore, many of them interactive. Some interpret the history of underwater exploration in the islands and some offer an unusual look at Bermuda's many shipwrecks. Others take a look at various types of underwater vehicles, including a full-size bathysphere as used by the indomitable Dr. Charles Beebe in 1934 while making his record breaking dive of more than 3,000 feet.

Also interesting is **Jack Lightbourn's** collection of more than 3,000 seashells. It is, perhaps, the most complete collection of its kind outside the great natural history museums of the world. Lightbourn began collecting seashells – like most of us do – as a child. But, unlike most of us, he didn't quit. He just kept on and on, gathering them from all corners of the world, until finally deciding to donate them to the institute.

Expect to spend two to three hours exploring the institute and museum. While there, take time out for a cup of java and a snack and don't miss the gift shops –

there are two – where you'll be sure to find that little something for the folks back home. The institute is wheelchair accessible, as are the restrooms. Hours are 10 am – 5 pm, Monday through Sunday, year-round (except Christmas Day). Admission is $11 for adults, $5.50 for children aged seven to 16; children six and under are free; $7.80 for seniors over 65.

Touring Sandy's Parish & the West End

The West End is a 45-minute ferry ride from Hamilton and about 35 minutes by bus.

Sandy's Parish (pronounced SANDS) is the barb of the hook-shaped island at the extreme western end of the Bermudian archipelago. It's the location of the historic Royal Naval Dockyard, now a unique mall full of interesting shops, pubs, restaurants and cafés.

The Village of Somerset is comprised of five small islands at the extreme west end of Bermuda: Somerset, Watford, Boaz, Ireland Island North, and Ireland Island South. Somerset is the largest of the five and, consequently, is the heart of the parish.

Somerset is named for Sir George Somers who greatly favored the West End, which for a time was known as Somers' Seate. It's mostly a rural area, with small farms and open spaces, craggy coastlines, tiny inlets, coves and wonderful beaches. This sleepy little fishing village has winding lanes, old fortifications, and waves that crash against the rocks on the ocean side, yet sit tranquil in the waters of the sound on the opposite side. All the attractions are set along the main road from Somerset Bridge on the southern boundary of the parish to the Royal Naval Dockyard on Ireland North. This layout makes touring the West End extremely easy. But Sandy's is best known for the Royal Naval Dockyard, and that's all most visitors ever see of the parish.

Sandy's Parish, Somerset and the West End are much more than the Dockyard, and you'll do well to make time for a proper visit; it can all be done in a day. Take either a bus or taxi to Somerset and begin at the southern end, or else jump on a ferry and start at the Dockyard.

Another option is renting a moped or bicycle. For variety, consider arriving one way and leaving by another. By bus from Hamilton (or from any stop along the way), go to Somerset Village and ask to get off at Somerset Bridge.

By moped or bicycle, head east on Front Street and follow the signs. When you reach the roundabout (a quaint old English improvement on the American four-way stop), you can either turn west on Harbour Road, or go on to the next roundabout and turn west onto South Road, following the coastline until it joins Middle Road. From there it's just a few more scenic miles to Somerset Bridge.

Somerset Bridge is unique because it's one of Bermuda's first three bridges, built in the 17th century, and also because it's the world's smallest drawbridge. At first glance, you'll find nothing unusual about the picturesque little bridge, but look more closely and you'll see the central plank can be raised, leaving a small opening just large enough for a sailboat mast to pass through.

From Somerset Bridge continue on to the Railway Trail (see full description). If you don't intend to hike the entire trail, simply take a stroll along the shady railway cut and enjoy splendid views of Great Sound.

Scaur Hill Fort Park is less than three-quarters of a mile down the road from Somerset Bridge. The fort was built on the highest hill on Somerset Island in the 1870s to protect Her Majesty's Royal Naval Dockyard in case of attack from

The sea, ostensibly by American forces. To defend the fort and Dockyard from an attack by land from the south, an enormous dry moat was dug that effectively cut Somerset in two. Any attack from that direction would have meant crossing not only the great moat, but surviving enfilading fire from cannon and rifle.

The fort is open to the public and serves as an excellent photographic opportunity. It stands in a 22-acre park complete with trails and picnic areas. The moat heads down to the shores of Great Sound, where you can spend time fishing or swimming. The fort itself is a massive stone-wall structure with many ramparts to wander around. Stand and look out across the sound toward Hamilton and you should be able to see the Dockyard away to your left. On a clear day with a telescope or binoculars, you might see St. David's Lighthouse or Fort St. Catherine, both at the extreme eastern end of the islands. Scaur Hill Fort and Fort Park is open daily from 9 am to 4:30 pm. Admission is free.

Return to the main road and head north a short distance to the Haydon Trust. The old chapel is thought to have been built around 1616. Visit the church and see the original oven in a small room behind the altar, a relic of the times when the building was a private residence. The grounds are well-kept, with a large lawn and several trails. The trust is open during daylight hours. Admission is free.

St. James' Church, 441-234-0834, stands on high ground and overlooks the ocean to the west. The church, the ocean and a magnificent sunset can provide an once-in-a-lifetime photo. Unfortunately, the original wooden church was destroyed in a hurricane in 1780. This replacement was consecrated in 1789; the iron gates were made by the Royal Engineers at the Dockyard in 1872, and the spire, added in 1880, was designed by Dr. Henry Hinson, a local physician who also designed spires for several other churches on the island. His spire was destroyed by lightning in 1937 and the one you see today is a faithful copy by Bermudian architect Will Onions. The church is open from dawn until dusk, and there's a tourist information center just a short distance away.

The Springfield & Gilbert Nature Reserve, 441-236-6483, is next. From St. James' Church stay on Somerset Road – the nature reserve is just a 10-Minute walk or a two-minute moped ride away. En route, you'll pass the Simmons Ice Cream Factory and Variety Store. Make it a point to stop and sample some of the best ice cream on the island. The nature reserve was once a Bermudian plantation built in the early 18th century. At the time of writing, the old house was undergoing extensive restoration, but the slave quarters, the buttery, and the mansion itself could still be viewed from the grounds. (By the time you read this, you should be able to visit inside.) A nature trail leads through more than five acres of unspoiled woodland and provides a quiet moment away from the beaches and crowds at the Dockyard. The reserve, a Bermuda National Trust property, is always open. Admission is free.

From the Springfield & Gilbert Nature Reserve, take Cambridge Road to **Somerset Long Bay Park and Nature Reserve**. The park, another one of Somerset's quiet places, has lots of appeal for the entire family.

You can snorkel, swim, picnic, walk or fish from the shore. The park was established by the Bermuda Audubon Society because the mangroves and the pond attract a variety of migrating birds both in the spring and in the fall. Warblers, kingfishers, cardinals, herons, egrets and ducks all take up residence here at one time or another.

The park is always open. Admission is free. Long Bay is also where you'll find most of Somerset's nicest beaches. The gorgeous sands of the Beach Park are to the north. At the eastern end of the bay is Daniel's Head, with **Daniel's Head Beach Park** to the southwest and the Sea Gardens, an underwater world full of marine life. One of Bermuda's best kept secrets.

Daniel's Head Beach Park, lies along 19 acres of the Atlantic shore. It seems a wild and remote spot. In times past it was host to the Canadian military, but they are long gone, leaving only the shells of the old barracks and recreation hall behind. It's one of those places the locals like to keep to themselves, and understandably so, beautiful and inviting, where the kids can swim in warm waters that are almost always calm and shallow.

It's also a great place for snorkelers as the waters teem with colorful angelfish, parrotfish, wrasse and sergeant majors. The two beaches are soft and white and ideal for the Sunday afternoon picnic – there's lots of room to cook-out and the sea on a sunny day is the color of uncut emeralds. It's a spot where lovers of the great outdoors can become one with nature, where you'll always find space to spread the blanket and just relax.

Remote as Daniel's Head is, it's not devoid of the necessities. There are public telephones, bathrooms and freshwater showers you can use for free, and there is always plenty of room to park the scooter. The park is on Daniel's Head Road, off Cambridge Road.

Somerset Village itself is a quiet little town of narrow streets, flowering hedges, tiny bays and brightly painted houses. Take a little time to explore the village and enjoy a cup of tea or a spot of lunch.

To the northwest, the village is bordered by Mangrove Bay, named for the trees along the shoreline, to the east by Great Sound, and a little farther to the southwest by Long Bay Beach. There are several shops to browse here, many of them smaller branches of those in Hamilton, as well as several pubs and restaurants. The main beach of Mangrove Bay is a picturesque area of blue waters and small boats bobbing at anchor, but it can – because of the traffic along the coast road – be somewhat noisy and dusty.

For a boat ride or for snorkeling over the reef, you'll find the Mangrove Bay wharf just a short way along Mangrove Bay Road. The management will gladly arrange whatever trip you feel like. Back in town at the Loyalty Inn, enjoy a cold beer or soft drink before continuing.

Lagoon Park is on Ireland Island South. As you leave Somerset Village and travel north along the main road and shoreline across Watford and Boaz Islands, you'll eventually come to Grey's Bridge. Cross the bridge and turn right onto Lagoon Road. (Now you're on the eastern shoreline.) Lagoon Park has a number of swimming and picnic areas, walking trails and a lake with all sorts of wild birds.

An Antidote for Yellow Fever Beyond Lagoon Park, after you rejoin the main road, you'll come to a very small bridge that spans a cut joining Great Sound to the ocean, dividing Ireland Island South from Ireland Island North. The cut was made for practical purposes. A doctor at the Royal Naval Hospital (which once stood on the hill overlooking the sound), found that he had more incidences of yellow fever at his hospital than at any other location on Bermuda.

After much deliberation, he had the cut made in order to reduce the "miasmas and vapors" emanating from the sound, and so reduced the number of yellow fever cases. A figment of old-time medical myth? You might think so, but in fact the changing tides cleansed the waters of mosquito larvae and, thus, yellow fever cases at the hospital dropped dramatically.

Just past the cut bridge, on your right, you'll find the Naval Cemetery, which dates from the early 19th century. Inside the graveyard are a number of interesting headstones, including those of four English admirals. The main road continues northward and eventually enters the main gates of the Royal Naval Dockyard. As you pass into the Dockyard, look up and to your left. The daunting structure rising above you is the old prison, still in use today. The Dockyard is just ahead.

Royal Naval Dockyard

The Royal Naval Dockyard, 441-234-3824, has had a long and often turbulent history. The American War of Independence brought the loss of English ports on the American mainland, but English interests in the area were far from finished. Pirates and privateers plied the waters, the French under Napoleon threatened English shipping routes to and from the West Indies, and then, of course, there were the Americans themselves.

The British Navy needed a major port and a dockyard capable of handling repairs to their warships. Bermuda

93

seemed to be the ideal location. Extensive surveys were carried out during the latter part of the 18th century and work began on the massive port project in 1809.

Photo Courtesy of the Bermuda Department of Tourism

The construction was done by thousands of slaves and English convicts under the direction of the Royal Corps of Engineers. The great breakwaters, the wharves, the boat slip, barracks, victualing yards, and the enormous fort took many, many years to complete. The unpaid laborers, working in the most appalling conditions, died by the thousands during this time.

For the next 150 years the Dockyard functioned as the British presence in the Western Atlantic. The great three-masted ships-of-the-line were replaced first by the steam-driven ironclads and then by the modern fleets we know today. Eventually, however, the need for the Dockyard dwindled and the Royal Naval

Dockyard closed for good in 1951. Even so, a visit here cannot fail to stir the blood. The massive structures, where generation after generation of British seamen lived out their traditions in the sunshine or in the shadow of the great fort, are silent now. Only fading images of the past remain among the crumbling structures.

Photo Courtesy of the Bermuda Department of Tourism

It might seem strange that one of Bermuda's oldest establishments is now its newest tourist attraction, but many of the old Dockyard buildings have been tastefully converted into shops, stores, restaurants and pubs. The Dockyard itself is a landscaped park with lawns and walks that stretch from one end to the other and along the water's edge. Aside from its shopping opportunities, the area is an extensive tourist center and yachting haven. Visitors by the hundreds arrive by bus, ferry and cruise ship to ride the tourist submarine Enterprise, the sightseeing helicopter, or visit the **Maritime Museum** housed in the nearby fortifications.

Of the buildings that remain structurally sound, the most impressive is the Clocktower Centre. The Clocktower Building, completed in 1856, is an exercise in architectural elegance and extravagance. The huge building has three-foot-thick walls and 100-foot-high twin towers. It was used as office space for the administration of naval stores. The clock on the south tower was cast in England in 1857 by John Moore & Sons. The matching clock on the north tower has just one hand that was set daily to indicate high-tide time (the safest time for seamen to navigate the reefs).

Today, the magnificent building has found new life as a shopping mall. The Clocktower Centre mall has 30 shops offering everything from antiques to gifts, old books to designer fashions. Even on the hottest summer days, the interior of this old building is cool – the massive walls have an insulating effect. For lunch or afternoon tea and sandwiches, try Pirates Landing, 441-234-5151. The shops in the Clocktower Centre are open daily from 10 am to 5 pm.

Beyond the center, take a short walk around the slip, where you can see boats being worked on. Farther along, you'll find the Victualing Yard and, beyond that, the old Cooperage and the Maritime Museum.

The Victualing Yard was the heart of naval operations within the Dockyard. It was here that food and supplies were prepared and stored. The yard is surrounded by a high, stone wall to keep supplies safe from pilferage. Today, it has become a park within a park. Where once hundreds of British seamen ran back and forth across the stone-flagged yard there are now trimmed lawns and benches surrounded by the ruins of massive stone warehouses.

Beyond the Victualing Yard is the Cooperage. In the days before refrigeration, the only way to preserve perishable goods like pork and biscuits was to salt them and seal them in barrels.

Photo Courtesy of the Bermuda Department of Tourism

With the many ships coming and going, a huge number of barrels were needed to handle the perishables at the Dockyard. These were made in the Cooperage, which was completed in 1831. Two large stone forges, used to make the iron hoops for the barrels, can be seen in the foyer of the cinema and at the English Pub.

The old Cooperage is now home of the Frog and Onion Pub and Restaurant, which has to be one of the most interesting culinary experiences on the island.For sure, it's the most authentic British pub in Bermuda. Most traditional English beers are available, along with shepherd's pie, steak and kidney pie, and beef and barley pie; add some good old English-style fish and chips – all great big portions – and you're in for a special experience. Better yet, it's not expensive; expect to pay between $10 and $20 per person, and that includes the price of a pint. Do I sound biased? You bet. 441-234-2900.

The Maritime Museum

The Maritime Museum, 441-234-1418, opened by Queen Elizabeth in 1975, is housed in the island's largest fortress, the one-time heart of the Dockyard's defenses. To enter the fortress, cross the wet moat by way of the drawbridge and pass under an archway in the massive stone wall. The Keep is a classic example of British military architecture. The walls are made from Bermuda limestone, the vaulted ceilings are lined with English brick, and the floors are coated with non-sparking bitumen. The massive ramparts are 30 feet high, with a water gate and an inner lagoon where small supply boats were loaded with munitions for the great ships-of the-line. As you walk the ramparts and explore the underground storage chambers, it's not difficult to imagine life within the fort all those years ago.

Royal Naval Dockyard Fortifications & Maritime Museum
Photo Courtesy of Aodhdubh and Creative Commons

The exhibits within the museum are varied and interesting. One display depicts shipwreck archaeology (there's certainly no shortage of wrecks) that includes recovered Spanish artifacts. There's also a fine collection of Bermuda boats in the Boat Loft, and "The Age of Discovery" exhibit celebrates the 500th anniversary of Christopher Columbus' discovery of the New World. Interesting, too, is the Bermuda Monetary Authority's section that traces the history of the island's currency from 1612 and the "Pillars of the Bridge" exhibit that celebrates the 50th anniversary of the establishment of the US naval bases on the island. Other displays deal with the Royal Navy, whaling, diving, navigation and shipping.

Best of all, however, is to stand high upon the ramparts and let your imagination wander back to a time when the grand three-masted warships rode at anchor in the sheltered waters of Great Sound. The Maritime Museum is open daily from 9:30 am to 4 pm, closed Christmas Day. Admission is $10 for adults, $8 for seniors and $5 for children ages five through 15; children under five are free if accompanied by an adult.

The Dockyard Snorkel Park

The Snorkel Park is fun for the whole family. You snorkel over marked underwater trails to view the underwater life that inhabits the Dockyard area. Floating stations along the way allow time out for a rest. Take your own equipment and the experience will cost you only $5 per person for as long as you like on any given day. Rent their equipment, however, and the cost is $17 for the day. I don't think that's too steep, considering the experience. Lifeguards are on duty and the park, located next to the Maritime Museum, is open from 10:30 am to 6 pm, Monday through Friday, and from 11 am to 5 pm over the weekend.

The park is closed November through March. 441-234-1006.

Royal Naval Dockyard Snorkel Park
Photo Courtesy of the Bermuda Department of Tourism

Gumba Trail & Outdoor Museum:

This is yet another neat attraction at the Royal Naval Dockyard, especially where kids are concerned. But take note that it can be enjoyed only on Wednesdays during the summer months, April through July. Special tours led by a Knowledgeable guide – the Gumba – explore the story behind the Caribbean Junkanoo dancers, as well as the various plants along the trail and their medicinal uses The hour-long tours are most interesting for the stories (many true), told by the Gumba. The cost is $5 per person. It's best to call ahead, too, especially if it looks like rain. 441-293-7330.

The Royal Naval Dockyard is also the place to enjoy jet skiing. Contact Wet and Wild for rates. 441-234-2426.

Dolphin Quest Bermuda.

The newest attraction in The Royal Naval Dockyard area is Dolphin Quest Bermuda. Once at what is now the Fairmont Southampton Princess Resort, Dolphin Quest has relocated to Sandy's Parish. All of the original interactive programs are still available, but there are now more members of the resident dolphin family and visitors are offered more time to get to know them.

The mammals seem to be extremely happy and comfortable, and they are certainly well-treated and looked after. They perform all the usual leaps and tricks. I've done the dolphin experience many times in many different locations; the tricks and the interactive programs are much the same wherever you might be, but it's worth doing again. The animals have unique personalities and there's always something new to learn. Also, I never tire of watching the kids get down and personal with these finny creatures. The animals seem to know that kids are special and they treat them as such. The last time we did it I bought the video tape. My daughter was 16 at the time and she had a whale of a time (no pun intended). We run that video now and again: great memories. Dolphin Quest Bermuda is at the Maritime Museum at the Royal Naval Dockyard.

Hours of operation are from 9:30 am until 4:30 pm daily, year-round. Wetsuits are available during the winter months. You'll need to pay the museum entrance fee of $7.50 for adults and $3 for children under 16. There's no charge for children under four. Dolphin Quest programs themselves start at around $25 per person. Give it a try; you won't be disappointed. 441-234-4464 or 800-248-3316. You can make reservations online at www.dolphinquest.org or email dqbermuda@dolphinquest.org. (It is recommended you make reservations before arriving in Bermuda, especially during peak season.)

When you've finished at the Royal Naval Dockyard, you'll face a decision: how to get back to Hamilton. If you arrived by moped and opt for the 45-minute ferry ride home, you'll be charged $3.50 extra to take the moped on board. But the ride across Great Sound is pleasant and worth the extra money. And you'll be tired after your visit so the rest, the salt spray, and a snack from the on-board concession bar will make for a very agreeable interlude.

Touring St. George's Parish

St. George is a 30-minute bus ride from Hamilton. Buses run between the town and Hamilton every 30 minutes, or every 15 minutes if you combine bus routes. At the other end of the island – the East End – is St. George's Parish. This is where it all started and where, today, you can visit those far off days when Sir George Somers and his friends on board the Sea Venture first hover into view off the tip of St. Catherine's Point.

A Walking Tour of St. George

The heart of the parish is the town of St. George. Founded in 1612 by Governor Sir George Moore and named for the patron saint of England, St. George was the second English town to be established in the New World after Jamestown, Virginia. Unlike Jamestown, though, which has long been abandoned, St. George continues its quiet way of life much as it has for almost four centuries.

As I've already mentioned, St. George is the oldest town in Bermuda. Indeed, with the demise of Jamestown in Virginia, it is the oldest English colonial settlement in the New World. For many years it was the capital of Bermuda, giving up that honor to the city of Hamilton in 1815. Today, St. George is a tiny backwater at the eastern end of the island. That's not to say it's a forgotten community, far from it. The little town is a major tourist attraction in its own right.

Over the years a great deal of history has been created on the streets of St. George and in the surrounding countryside. The harbor has offered food and shelter to more than 20 generations of seafarers. Many of them saw Bermuda as no more than a small spot on the map of the journey to the New World.

The St. George of today is a tiny community, clean and neat, with dozens of quaint shops and stores, side streets and long sloping sidewalks.

You'll need to take your time when exploring St. George. If you can, allow at least a full day, more if possible, because here you'll be treated to more old English and Bermudian tradition than anywhere else on the islands. Allow time to explore the quaint little shops and stores where the unexpected is always just around the corner, or hidden away in some dark recess waiting just for you to discover it. If you have the time and energy you should make the walk from St. George to Fort St. Catherine; it's almost a couple of miles, but the walk is fun, and the fort itself is not to be missed; just take your time. You can catch a bus from the fort back into town.

The tour of St. George I've laid out is quite comprehensive, taking in almost all the major sights of the city, and one or two spots that are not quite so obvious attractions. The tour can take as much as a full day, the fort a half-day, so allow plenty of time, and bring some extra cash to spend along the way. Begin your tour of the parish in King's Square, also known over the years as the Market Square and the King's Parade.

The Visitors Service Bureau here, 441-297-1642, is open 9 am to 5 pm every day except Sunday.

King's Square is the hub of the town. On any given day almost every resident of St. George will pass through it or spend some time there. During the summer months it's a lively place. The Town Crier, in 17th-century costume, can often be seen ringing his bell and calling out the events of the day. As soon as you enter on the north side of the square, you'll see the town stocks, whipping posts and pillories just to your left. These offer an unusual photographic opportunity.

There's also a ducking stool in the square, which once was used to punish female gossips; it was, to say the least, a harrowing experience for the lady concerned. Strange as it may seem, the men were never treated to the experience.

King's Square
Photo Courtesy of the Bermuda Department of Tourism

Today, St. George's town crier, Richard Olsen, announces the punishments for the day: reenactments of those long since abandoned, including the ducking stool. **King's Square** is also the site of most of St. George's annual celebrations: New Years, Emancipation Day, etc., and an assortment of outdoor concerts held throughout the year.

The **White Horse Tavern** is a welcoming place to enjoy a pint of beer, lunch, and a magnificent view of the harbor and The Deliverance. There's a visitor information center on the south side of the square at the water's edge. Here you'll find all the information you'll need about St. George and its surroundings, and more: excursions, day trips, bus schedules, pamphlets and brochures, shopping, dining, and so on. You can even buy bus tickets at the Bureau. The Bureau is open April through October from 9 am to 1 pm, and from 1:30 to 4 pm, Monday through Saturday. During the winter months, November through March, the hours are from 9 am until 2 pm, Monday through Saturday. 441-297-1642.

The Globe Hotel and Bermuda National Trust Museum:

The old hotel was open to guests in the early to mid-19th century, but its history goes all the way back to when it was built by Bermuda's governor, Samual Day, in 1699, making it one of the oldest buildings on the islands. It hasn't seen a paying guest in many a long year.

Today, however, it entertains paying guests of a different kind: it's a National Trust property housing a number of artifacts and exhibits that faithfully interpret the history of the islands in general and St. George in particular. These include a replica of the Sea Venture and a movie titled Bermuda: Centre of the Atlantic. On the upper floor you can see an exhibit called Rogues and Runners: Bermuda and the American Civil War. But the Globe's connections to the American Civil War go much deeper than the exhibit. During those days of blockades and gunrunners a Confederate agent actually had an office in the building. The museum is open year-round, except for public holidays, from 10 am until 4 pm, Monday through Saturday. Admission is $5. 441-297-1423.

From King's Square you'll naturally wander in the direction of the harbor and cross the bridge onto Ordnance Island. There, you'll find not only a wonderful view of King's Square and St. George, but a couple of unique points of interest. The first, and you can't fail to see it, is a full-size replica of **The Deliverance**. The Deliverance, along with a second ship, The Patience, was built from the wreckage of Sir George's flagship, Sea Venture. In 1610, the survivors of the wreck continued their journey to the New World and eventually arrived safely in Jamestown. Looking at the replica of The Deliverance it's difficult to believe that men and women set sail in such tiny vessels, often for months at a time, at the mercy of wind and weather. Would you? 441-297-1459.

Stop 2 on your tour is just across the way to the east. The statue of **Admiral Sir George Somers** stands in a small landscaped garden at the water's edge. It depicts a flamboyant, happy-go-lucky individual very much in keeping with what one might expect in an adventurer of his class.

Back across the bridge on the west side of King's Square is **St. George's Town Hall** (Stop 3), 441-297-1532. There's a small theater on the top floor where you can view an audiovisual presentation of The Bermuda Journey (Stop 4), the story of Bermuda and its people. The Town Hall is the meeting place for the Town Corporation, a body of three aldermen and five councilors headed by the mayor. The sedate old building has seen some exciting times, not the least of which was its siege by English soldiers, under orders from the Royal Governor to arrest the mayor, who had taken refuge inside. The Town Hall is open Monday through Saturday from 10 am until 4 pm.

Stop 5 is **the Bridge House**, 441-297-8211. Walk a short distance from King's Square up King Street; Bridge House is on the left. Built sometime around 1700, the house was home to several of Bermuda's early governors and of Virginia loyalist, Bridger Goodrich, who fled the colony during the American War of Independence. Goodrich was an adventurer of the first order. Arrogant, resourceful and ruthless, he organized a fleet of privateers and blockaded Chesapeake Bay, destroying all who traded with the American enemy. These, unfortunately, included Bermudian vessels. They fell prey to Goodrich's privateers, a fact that did not endear him to the Bermudian people. Bridge House is now an art gallery and private apartments owned by the Bermuda National Trust. The house is open Monday through Saturday from 10 am until 5 pm.

A little farther east along King Street is the State House (Stop 6), 441-297-8211. This is the oldest building in Bermuda. Built in 1620 by Governor Nathaniel Butler in the Italian style, it was the House of Assembly and the location of the principle court during the time when St. George was Bermuda's capital.

Today, the house is leased to a Masonic lodge for an annual rent of one peppercorn per year. The ceremony of payment is held in April and has become one of the town's major celebrations. The State House is open to the public on most Wednesdays from 10 am until 4 pm.

North of the **State House**, across Duke of York Street, are the Somers' Gardens, Stop 7. This is where Sir George Somers' heart and entrails were buried; his body was sent back to England. When Sir George finally arrived in Jamestown he found only 60 of the colonists still alive. The winter period of 1609-1610 in Jamestown's history became known as the "Starving Time." No sooner had Somers arrived than he took a ship back to Bermuda in search of food and supplies for the starving colony. This was to be his last voyage; he died shortly after arriving in Bermuda. The gardens, opened in 1920 by the Duke of Windsor, then the Prince of Wales, feature tropical flowers, shrubs and trees. Open daily from 8 am until 4 pm.

Continue your walk through Somers' Gardens up the steps to the North Gate onto Blockade Alley. On the hill is the **Unfinished Church**, Stop 8. The church is something of an enigma. Now very much in ruins, it was designed to replace St. Peter's but, unfortunately, was never finished. Soon after construction began in the 1870s, the project was beset by financial difficulties, the work slowed, and then stopped altogether. Finally, after a storm did more damage than could easily be repaired, it was abandoned. The end of the new church, however, brought a new beginning to the old one; it's a fine building you'll visit later on your tour.

Turn south on Duke of Kent Street and walk to the corner of Featherbed Alley, where you'll find the **St. George's Historical Society Museum** (Stop 9), 441-297-0423. This is a fine example of 18th-century Bermudian architecture. Exhibits include the original kitchen, many examples of antique and period furniture, a collection of old documents and paintings, and a rare Bible. The museum is open on Tuesdays, Wednesdays and Thursdays from 10 am A section of the Unfinished Church until 4 pm. Admission is $5 for adults, and $2 for children aged six to 16; children under the age of six are free.

Just around the corner from the Historical Society Museum, on Featherbed Alley, is Stop 10, Featherbed Alley Printery. The little shop has a printing machine of the type invented by Johannes Gutenburg in the 1450s. This interesting place is open from 10 am until 4 pm, Monday through Saturday (closed from 11 am until 2 pm on Wednesday and Thursday).

Stop 11 is The Old Rectory, 441-297-4261. Continue on Featherbed Alley to Church Street. The Old Rectory is just to the right on Broad Alley. The house was once the home of Parson Richardson, the rector of St. Peter's from 1755 to 1805, nicknamed "The Little Bishop." It was built in 1705 by a reformed pirate. Today, the neat little house is a private residence owned by the Bermuda National Trust. It's open on Wednesday from noon until 5 pm. Admission is free.

St. Peter's Church, 441-297-8359, is Stop 12 on your map. From Broad Alley and the Old Rectory, you can reach it through the back entrance into the churchyard, which is opposite Broad Alley on Church Lane. The old churchyard is filled with headstones, some of which date back well over 300 years. St. Georgians and Bermudians of all walks of life are buried here. There are governors, professionals, ordinary townsfolk, pirates and, perhaps best-known, there's the grave of Midshipman Richard Dale. Dale was an American seaman who was mortally wounded during a sea battle with the English in the War of 1812. He was 20 years old when he died in 1815. The monument you see here was erected by his parents in tribute to the people of St. George because their "tender sympathy prompted the kindest attentions to their son while living and honored him when dead."

To the west of the church you'll find the graves of a number of slaves. The cedar tree you see by the back entrance is more than 500 years old and the church bell once hung from its branches.

St. Peter's is the oldest continually used Anglican Church in the Western Hemisphere, and parts of it do date back to 1620, but it's not the original one; it's not even the second one. The first church was built on the site in 1612. It was a wooden affair with a palmetto thatched roof. That was replaced by a more permanent stone structure in 1619 when it was severely damaged during a storm. In turn, the second church was almost entirely replaced by the present church in 1713; the tower was added in 1814.

The church was, until the building of the State House in 1620, the new colony's only meeting place. It was here that the first assizes were held in 1616 and the Bermuda Parliament met for the first time in 1620. There's a guide on duty during the week who will explain the history, but you can also wander around on your own.

The altar is the oldest piece of woodwork on the island. It was carved by Richard Moore, who was a shipwright and Bermuda's first governor.

The font is believed to be at least 500 years old and was brought to the island by the first colonists.

The three-tier pulpit dates to the early 17th century and the galleries on either side of the church were added in 1833.

Be sure to look at the wall memorials; some of the names are quite amusing.

The vestry displays the fine silver collection, which includes a beautiful Charles I chalice that came over from England in 1625 and a communion set from 1697. The church is open daily and for Sunday service. Admission is free, but donations are appreciated.

Leave St. Peter's by the front door and walk down the steps to Duke of York Street. Turn right, pass the police station in the next block and turn left onto **Barber's Alley**. This alley is named for a black freeman, Hayne Rainey, of South Carolina. During the American Civil War, he escaped to Bermuda on board a blockade runner. A self-educated man, he spent his time on the island barbering. When he eventually returned to America, he was elected to Congress – the first black member of the House of Representatives.

Continue down Barber's Alley to Water Street and turn right to Stop 13, The **Tucker House Museum**, 441-297-0545; it's just around the corner on the right side of Water Street. The house, built in 1711, is owned by the Bermuda National Trust and is an encapsulated history of the Tucker family, still an important presence on the islands. Edward "Teddy" Tucker is a diver, treasure hunter and historian of international reputation, and is something of a legend here. In days gone by members of the family have included a Governor of Bermuda, a United States Treasurer, a Confederate Navy Captain and an Episcopal Bishop.

The museum is a treasure house filled with antiques, artifacts and memorabilia, including a collection of Bermudian cedar furniture, many fine portraits, and antique silver. In addition, there's an interesting collection of items that were discovered beneath the cellar floor. The museum is open Monday through Saturday from 9:30 am until 4:30 pm, April until October, and from 10 am until 4 pm, November through March. Admission is $5.

Rogues & Runners, 441-297-1423. This building was erected in 1700 by Governor Samuel Day. During his administration he claimed the house as his own and initiated a court case that he was never to see the end of. Day died in prison and never knew that his claim was successful. The building served for more than half its existence as the Globe Hotel.

During the American Civil War it was the office of Confederate Agent, Major Norman Walker. Walker chose St. George because of its sympathy to the Southern cause, more for economic than ideological reasons. St. George, still trying to recover from the depression caused by the removal of the capital to Hamilton in 1815, had become the center for blockade running activities on the islands. Inside the museum you find a number of interesting Confederate artifacts, including a replica of the Great Seal of the Confederacy and an antique machine which will make a reproduction of the seal for you to take home as a souvenir.

The house, owned by the Bermuda National Trust, is open Monday through Saturday, 9:30 am until 4:30 pm from April until October, and 10 am until 4 pm, November through March. Admission is $4. That just about concludes your tour of St. George itself, but no visit would be complete without stopping at Fort St. Catherine and the much smaller, but no less interesting, Gates Fort to the south.

Fort St. Catherine

Stop 16 on the map, 441-297-1920, is about two miles from the town of St. George on the extreme eastern tip of the island known as St. Catherine's Point. If the walk is a little too much, you can jump on a bus. There should be one going by every 30 minutes or so. Built as part of the islands' defensive system, the fort has been restored to its original state and contains underground chambers and tunnels carved deep into the bedrock, cannon, guns, a number of military exhibits, and replicas of the Crown Jewels. There are also interesting dioramas depicting the islands' past and a video presentation that tells the history of Bermuda's forts.

The area surrounding the fort is popular for picnicking and recreation. The beaches are quiet and clean, and provide excellent opportunities for swimming and snorkeling.

Fort Dt. Catherine - Photo Courtesy of the Bermuda Department
of Tourism

The fort itself, with its massive walls, ramparts, and tiny nooks and crannies, is a photographer's dream come true. It is open daily from 10 am until 4:30 pm. Admission is $5; children ($2) must be accompanied by an adult.

The last four stops on your tour of St. George's involve a bus ride.

Stop 17 is **Gates Fort**, right at the end of Cut Road on the tip on the peninsula. Take a number 3 bus outward- bound; it's a one-mile ride or an easy walk. The scenery along the way is spectacular. If you walk, take Barrack Road to the end of Cut Road, where you'll find the fort. You can visit any time you like; there are no formal hours. It's worthwhile to make the climb of the keep, if only for the view of the channel. There are also a couple of large guns up there that will provide an interesting photo opportunity.

Gates Fort is a reconstruction of a small redoubt that was built on this site in the early 1600s. At one time it was a private home. The fort itself is not much, but the sea and shore are beautiful. If you've brought along a picnic, this is the place to eat it. Gates Fort is open daily and no admission is charged.

To reach Stop 18 you'll need to return to St. George's and take a number 6 bus out to St. David's Lighthouse, 441-297-1642. (You'll pass Stop 19, The **Carter House**, along the way, but don't worry, you'll see it on the return trip.) The small community of St. David's, apart from the naval base there, is one of the wildest and most remote spots on the islands. The locals, so islanders say, live in a world all their own. Some of the residents have supposedly never even been as far "abroad" as St. George's.

The **lighthouse at St. David's** is set at the highest point on the eastern coast. It stands 208 feet above sea level and was built in 1879 of Bermuda limestone. From the balcony high above St. David's Head, you'll enjoy spectacular views of the surrounding countryside, the Atlantic Ocean to the south, Ruth's Bay to the southwest, the South Shore, and St. David's and St. George's to the north. If you saw the movie, The Deep, you'll be interested to learn that this is the lighthouse they used in the story. You'll also recall that they blew it up at the end of the movie. Well, of course, the one they destroyed was only a replica; neat! The lighthouse is open most days during the summer, but call ahead to check, 441-297-1642.

From St. David's, hop aboard another number 6 bus and head back in the direction of St. George's. Stop 19 is the Carter House, located inside the naval base; ask the driver to drop you off at the main gate.

The **Carter House** is one of the oldest homes in Bermuda. It was built in 1640 by the descendants of Christopher Carter, one of three men left behind on the islands when The Deliverance and The Patience sailed for Jamestown and the New World in 1610.

Christopher Carter

Carter was apparently something of a rogue. While waiting for the ships to return from Jamestown, he and two other men discovered a cache of ambergris – an expensive product of the sperm whale used in making perfume – washed up on the beach. The three men conspired in what became known as the "Ambergris Plot" to smuggle the stuff back to England, where they planned to sell it. But Carter got cold feet and, when the ships pulled into the harbour, he turned his co-conspirators in to Governor Moore. Carter remained on the islands and eventually settled on Cooper's Island, now a part of the naval base.

The old house built by Carter's descendants has been restored almost to its colonial condition. The interior houses antique furniture, artifacts and memorabilia, including a fine old tavern table. The Carter House is open on Wednesdays from 10 am until 3 pm and admission is free. Stop at the main gate of the naval station and show a photo ID. You might want to call ahead and double-check the opening times, 441-297-1642.

The final stop, Stop 20, is the Bermuda Biological Station for Research. Take a number 6 bus from the Carter House and ask the driver to drop you off at Ferry Reach, or take a number 1, 3, 10 or 11 bus inbound to Hamilton from St. George's and, again, get off at Ferry Reach.

Scientists at the research station have been studying marine life since 1903. The facilities are extensive and have been the subject of several novels, the best-known of which was Beast by Peter Benchley of Jaws fame. The story, although somewhat out of this world, gives some good insight as to the goings-on at the facility.

Bermuda Biological Station
Photo Courtesy of the Bermuda Department of Tourism

The station has its own deep-water ocean research ship, 13 laboratories, a 250-seat lecture hall and an extensive library. Guided tours of the facilities and grounds are conducted on Wednesdays at 10 am. There's no charge for the tour, which includes coffee and donuts, but donations are welcome. 441-297-1880.

Your tour of St. George's Parish has touched only the highlights; there's much more for you to see and do. Shopping in this little community is good and varied, but on a smaller scale than Hamilton. There are a number of restaurants and several tiny back-street and courtyard shopping areas with flowers, trees and benches.

If you don't manage to see everything in one day, a return visit is easy enough as buses run back and forth between Hamilton and St. George from early in the morning until late in the evening.

Touring the Other Parishes:

The remaining six parishes on Bermuda form a chain that runs east to west. To tour them you will need to rent a moped or a bicycle, or take advantage of the bus and ferry system. Following is a round-up, parish-by-parish, of the most interesting attractions. Be prepared to exercise a little flexibility during your tour. Who knows what you'll find around the next bend or down that tiny side road? The island is not a big one, and there's plenty of time for side trips.

It's not feasible to tour all six parishes in a single day. So I've divided the tour into three sections, each planned for a day of exploring. If you decide to use public transport, be prepared to do a little walking. There's nothing too far off the beaten path and most of the tour stops are just a pleasant stroll away from the bus routes. As you'll be making frequent stops, it is highly recommended that you buy one of the three- or seven-day passes. A pass is convenient and will save you a great deal of money. Don't worry too much about schedules. The beauties of the Bermudian Public Transport System are its convenience, frequency and the short distances between stops. You can jump off the bus just about anywhere, secure in the knowledge that there will be another bus along in 30 minutes or less. If you decide you'd like to do the tour by moped or bicycle, the following directions will work just as well for you.

Touring Southampton Parish

A great way to start your tour is on the ferry from Hamilton to Somerset. Ferries leave the dock in Hamilton at 9 and 10 am. The 9 am ferry goes via the Naval Dockyard and arrives at Somerset Bridge Wharf at 10:15. The later ferry goes direct to Somerset and reaches its destination in just 30 minutes. From the wharf, you can take a bus east on Middle Road into Southampton Parish. On your return trip, catch either a number 8 bus that will take you all the way back to Hamilton via Middle Road, or a number 7 that will take you to Hamilton via the scenic South Shore and the beaches.

Remember that bus stops along the routes are marked by pink and blue poles. Those poles with a pink section at the top indicate the stops for Hamilton-bound buses; those with a blue section at the top are outward-bound from Hamilton. To stop a bus you must stand by the pole. In places it might seem dangerous to do this, so always exercise extreme caution and be on the lookout for fast-moving traffic.

If you're going by moped or bicycle you can ride out to Somerset Bridge Wharf and follow the route, or you can take your rental with you on the ferry; it will cost an extra $3.50. Assuming you've arrived at Somerset Bridge Wharf by ferry, you can grab either a number 7 or number 8 bus going east to Hamilton. From Somerset Bridge Wharf, you'll travel east for about two miles to Whale Bay Road. Have the driver stop there and let you off. From Middle Road, walk down Whale Bay Road for about 700 yards. At the end you'll find a secluded, rocky little bay with a pink-tinged sandy beach and crystal-clear waters overlooked by Whale Bay Fort, Stop 1 on your tour.

The tiny fort – it's more of a battery than a fort – is overgrown now, but it's a pleasant spot where wildflowers and tropical plants grow in showy profusion. If you came by moped or bicycle you'll have to leave it behind and walk down to the beach; it's accessible only on foot. If you've brought along your swimming gear, now might be a good time to get changed and go for a dip in the ocean; you won't find a better place.

From Whale Bay Fort, walk back up Whale Bay Road, catch a number 7 bus, and continue eastward to Lighthouse Road. You'll travel about a mile to a point where the road forks and turns southward to the coast road and the beaches. Lighthouse Road is 2½ miles from Whale Bay Road.

As you travel along South Road you'll pass by many of the best beaches on the islands. Stop the bus any time you feel like exploring. Leave the bus at Church Road and spend some time on the beach in the public park at Church Bay, and then stroll along the road going eastward to Lighthouse Road. It's a walk of a little more than a mile. Along the way, on the right, you'll pass by the Reefs Hotel at Christian Bay and the old Sonesta Beach Hotel a little farther on. Look down from the cliff tops to the sea and the beaches; the views are wonderful. Be sure to take your camera!

Gibbs Hill Lighthouse

When you get off the bus you'll turn left onto Lighthouse Road and walk for a couple of hundred yards or so up the hill to Gibbs Hill Lighthouse (Stop 2), 441-238-8069 or 238-5703.

This magnificent lighthouse is one of the oldest of its kind in the world. Built of cast iron, its construction started in England in 1844. The plates were shipped to Bermuda and assembled on the site. At 117 feet tall, it stands on a hill 245 feet above sea level for a combined 362 feet; it's one of the highest spots on the islands.

The original lamp at Gibbs Hill was a great wick and oil affair. Today, its 1,000-wattbulb casts a beam of light that can, on a clear day, be seen by ships more than 40 miles out to sea. Aircraft can see it from more than 120 miles away. In times past it relied upon its rotating reflectors to attract the attention of ships that strayed too close to the rocks. These days the beam is locked onto wayward vessels by radar. There's a small souvenir shop in the building at the foot of the tower where you can purchase gifts, T-shirts and such. The grounds are well kept and a pleasant place to stroll or sit for a while.

Now, how about a trip to the top? If you decide to take it on, you'll negotiate a spiral staircase of 185 steps. It's not a climb for the faint-hearted, but the view is worth the exertion (there are stops along the way where you can rest and catch your breath). The balcony offers a spectacular all-around view of Bermuda. If you have a problem with heights, however, stay on the ground. The tower sways slightly in the wind and the balcony is narrow, with only a guard rail between you and the ground 127 feet below. After your climb to the top and back down again, a little light refreshment will definitely be welcome. If so, there's no better place to get it than in the Lighthouse Tearoom. Here, for less than $15, you can enjoy an old-fashioned English cream tea for two: scones, butter and clotted cream, along with a generous pot of tea. If you're an early bird, you can take breakfast in the Tearoom, and that's another culinary experience you won't want to miss.

The Tearoom is open Monday through Saturday from 9 am until 5 – yes, they serve lunch as well – and on Sundays from 2 pm until 4:30. If you collect miniature lighthouses and related paraphernalia, you must drop in at the gift shop where you'll find all sorts of interesting bits and pieces, as well T-shirts and other assorted souvenirs. The lighthouse is open daily from 9 am until 4:30 pm. Admission is $2.50. If you have a bus pass, admission is free.

Stop 3, South Shore Park, is just a little farther along the road to the east. From the lighthouse, walk back down the hill to South Road, where you can either grab a bus or turn left and walk for about a mile to South Shore Park on your right. You'll see the bays and beaches from your vantage point on the road high above. Photographers should take advantage of the far-reaching views here.

From South Road, walk down the winding road to the park and Horseshoe Bay, the first of a long line of bays and beaches that stretches eastward for more than four miles through Warwick Parish to Elbow Beach in Paget. Before you leave the road, however, you might like to try Tio Pepe's, 441-238-1897, and a neat roadside eatery close to the entrance of Horseshoe Bay. You can have lunch there and they also offer food to go. They serve good Italian cuisine and their pizza might be just what you need for a picnic on the beach.

It's very easy for a writer to get carried away when describing the South Shore. The area must be one of the most beautiful vacation spots in the world. From Horseshoe Bay, the pinkish sand and the vast turquoise ocean seems to stretch to infinity. The waves, always heavier on this side of the island, surge over the beaches and in and out of the rocky inlets and secluded coves. In one spot it might be easy to believe you are on the rocky coastline of Scotland, in another you could be on the beach in Florida. Each tiny section of the South Shore is unique.

Horseshoe Bay is perhaps the best known of the South Shore beaches. The great crescent of sand and sea stretches for several hundred yards and can, at peak periods, become extremely crowded. It's the place as far as Bermudians are concerned, the center of the islands' weekend social scene. Locals flock to Horseshoe for the sun, sand and sea. It's also the place where the local teenagers hang out. And it's one of two beaches on the islands where there are lifeguards on duty during the summer – the other is John Smith's Bay in Smith's Parish, way off to the east.

Even though there are lifeguards, you'll need to be careful of the undertow, which can be severe on windy days; keep a sharp eye on your youngsters.

There are public toilets and a snack bar. At either end of the bay, rocky outcrops offer a tempting opportunity to go climbing. If you do, be sure to stay on the well-worn paths. A fall from the top could put an end to your vacation.

At this point you can either go back to the road and head east (although a bus is not really necessary) or you can walk along the beach. Back on the road you'll turn right and walk for about a quarter-mile before turning left onto Camp Hill Road. Here you'll find Warwick Camp. You are now in Warwick Parish.

Touring Warwick Parish

Warwick Camp, Stop 4, was built just after the end of the Civil War. It was supposed to guard the beaches against an enemy landing. That, of course, never happened. During World War I it was used as a training ground and rifle range. Pearl White shot a movie here in the 1920s. Today, it's a quiet place where you can relax and enjoy the view. Stop 5, Christ Church, is a little out of your way but, if you like old churches, it's worth a visit. Built in 1719, it's the oldest Presbyterian Church in the British Commonwealth. From Camp Hill Road, turn east on South Road, go to Tribe Road 7 and make a right. Walk a half-mile or so to Middle Road then catch a bus to the Belmont Hotel; the church is just across the road. If you decided to give Christ Church a miss, from Warwick Camp you can return to South Road, and from there to the beaches.

Photo Courtesy of Bermuda Department of Tourism

Jobson's Cove

Stop 6, Jobson's Cove, is just 100 yards or so farther east. The cove is one of the most appealing spots on the island. Though secluded and often deserted during the winter, it can become a little crowded at other times, and it doesn't take many people to achieve that. If you visit when it's not crowded, you'll be able to leave the world behind. The rocky cliffs hem in the tiny beach and, even though you're only yards away from civilization, you'll experience a feeling of total isolation, even loneliness. It's a great spot for swimming or snorkeling. Visit the cove late at night, say midnight, and don't be surprised if you find people skinny-dipping!

Warwick Long Bay

From Jobson's Cove, you can stay on the beach and walk east along the shoreline to Stop 7, Warwick Long Bay. Viewed from the water the half-mile long, pink-tinged sandy beach at Warwick Long Bay is, as the name implies, the longest and straightest continuous stretch of beach on Bermuda. In the early mornings, when there's a soft sea mist, you won't be able to see the end of it. Warwick Long Bay is protected from the big breakers by the inner reef and the sea is almost always calm. It is popular and sometimes crowded, but never uncomfortably so. There's plenty of room for all. The beach itself is backed by steep, rocky cliffs and sandy hills covered with sea grass and scrub. It's a combination, along with a huge rock that sticks up out of the ocean some 100 yards offshore that offers photographers unique and interesting opportunities.

Warwick Long Bay
Photo Courtesy of Bermuda Department of Tourism

Stop 8 on your tour is Astwood Park. To reach it you can either continue your walk eastward along the beach – it's about a mile – or return to the road and take the bus. Astwood Park is a pleasant public area with flowers, shrubs, a number of picnic tables and a couple of beaches; just the place for a rest or a swim.

Touring Paget Parish

Paget Parish is a good place to start or end your day of sightseeing. You can either jump on a bus – a number 7 or 8 will get you where you want to go – or you can take the ferry from Hamilton over to one of the three docks in Paget: Lower Ferry Landing, Hodson's Ferry or Sea Kettle Wharf. Lower Ferry Landing will probably suit you best. Paget is one of the most popular parishes in Bermuda. On one side it's bordered by the ocean, on the other by Hamilton Harbour. The view across the harbor to the city is a spectacular one. In the early evening, just after dark, the lights and the floodlit cathedral are an eye-popping sight.

The first stop of the day (Stop 9) is Clermont. It's just a short walk from the ferry landing on Harbour Road. This fine old house is not open to the public, but it's not out of your way and is worth stopping by to look. Once the home of Sir Brownlow Grey, the Chief Justice of Bermuda, it is noted for its fine and extensive woodwork. Clermontis also famous as the site of Bermuda's first tennis court. Mary Outerbridge, on a visit from New York in 1874, learned to play tennis at Clermont and, on her return to the United States, she introduced the game to America.

From Clermont, walk west a short distance and turn left onto Valley Road, where you'll find Stop 10, St. Paul's Church. St. Paul's was built in 1796 to replace an earlier church. Its claim to fame is the ghost which was said to haunt the area for a short time around the turn of the century.

The Ghost of St. Paul's

Never seen, but often clearly heard – the soft sound of tinkling bells – the ghost was diligently hunted by locals. The hunt became something of a media event, if there was such a thing in those days, with local vendors setting up refreshment stands. In the end, however, an American scientist solved the mystery by attributing the strange sounds to a rare bird: the filio. But did he solve the mystery? The bird was never seen here and the sounds continued, at least for a while. Then, one day, the ghost was gone, and it has never been heard from since.

Stop 11, Paget Marsh, is right next door to St. Paul's on Middle Road. Paget Marsh has been preserved by the Bermuda National Trust to show what the islands must have been like when the first settlers arrived. The 18-acre tract of unspoiled woodland reserve features many of the islands' endangered plants and shrubs, along with a variety of trees, including cedars, palmetto and mangrove. If you want to look around the marsh you'll need to give the National Trust a call before you make your visit. They are very accommodating and will be happy to make the arrangements, 441-236-6483.

Botanical Gardens

From Paget Marsh, return to Valley Road and walk south to Middle Road, grab an inbound bus – stand on the left side of the road at one of the poles with a pink section at the top – and go east for about a mile to the Botanical Gardens, Stop 12, 441-236-4201. The driver will be happy to drop you off at the right spot. Alternatively, you can walk; it's quite a pleasant stroll. Walk east along Harbour Road to the roundabout, where you'll find Point Finger Road to your right, Front Street to your left, and Berry Hill Road and the Botanical Gardens opposite.

The gardens form a magnificent 36-acre landscaped park where tiny paths meander among a profusion of exotic tropical plants, flowers and trees. There's an aviary; a hibiscus garden with more than 150 varieties; and a special garden for the blind, filled with all sorts of fragrant plants and flowers – lavender, lemon, geranium, spices. The lawns are thick and green and there are a number of ruined stone buildings covered with vines; there's even a miniature forest. In the main building you'll find a visitor center where you can obtain information to guide you through the gardens, including a nature guide. There's also a tea room, a gift shop, and the offices of the Bermuda Department of Agriculture.

Be prepared to spend quite a bit of time here. The gardens are extensive and a full tour will take at least an hour and a half. You can wander around independently or you can take a guided tour, which leaves the visitor center at 10:30 am on Tuesday, Wednesday and Friday through the summer months, and Tuesday and Friday only from November through March. The gardens are open daily from sunrise to sunset and admission is free.

Stop 13 is within the grounds of the Botanical Gardens. Camden, the official residence of Bermuda's Prime Minister, is open only on Tuesday and Friday. Even when it's not open, you can peek in the windows. Admission is free.

Touring Devonshire Parish

Devonshire Parish, bordered by Paget, Pembroke and Smith's Parish, offers more peace and quiet than almost anywhere else on the island. There are no hotels and few restaurants. If you need a bite to eat, try the Specialty Inn; it's a half-mile east of Stop 16 on South Shore Road. They serve a good lunch or breakfast there, and it's not expensive. From the Botanical Gardens go to Berry Hill Road and turn right. Walk to Tee Street, turn left and go to Middle Road.

Turn right there and go a half-mile to Stop 14, The Old Devonshire Church. The church you see is not the original, although it stands on the site where the first church was built in 1612. The second church, built in 1716, was destroyed in an explosion in 1970. The church you see before you is a faithful reproduction of that one. It's more like a cottage than a church, but a church it is, and a very popular one too. The pews, the communion table and the pulpit apparently came from the original church of 1612. The church silver is the oldest on the island, some pieces dating to the late 16th century. Old Devonshire is open daily from 9 am until 5:30 pm and admission is free.

From the Old Devonshire Church, turn south onto Brighton Hill Road and walk for about three-quarters of a mile to South Shore Road, where you'll find the Palm Grove Gardens (Stop 15).Palm Grove is an 18-acre estate of landscaped gardens, the main feature of which is the pond, with its landscaped relief map of Bermuda. Each parish is picked out in the close-cropped map of grass. It's different and it's fun. Palm Grove is open Monday through Thursday from 9 am until 5 pm and admission is free.

From Palm Grove, return to South Shore Road and walk east for a short distance to a small side road leading off to the right. You'll see a sign pointing the way to Devonshire Bay Park and Devonshire Bay Battery, Stop 16.

Devonshire Bay is a quiet place, often deserted, always pleasant – a good spot to spend some time picnicking, swimming, or just relaxing and watching the ocean and the sea birds swooping and diving. You'll probably need a rest after all the walking you've done to get here! The battery, a small fort, was once a part of the islands' defensive system. It's now a somewhat lonely place on a site overlooking the bay. Bring your camera. At the end of the day you can return to South Shore Road and grab a number 1 bus back to Hamilton.

Touring Smith's Parish

From Hamilton, take a number 1 bus going to St. George's or Grotto Bay – there's one leaving every 30 minutes from 6:45 am onward, Monday through Friday, from 8:15 am on Saturday, and every hour from 11 am on Sunday. Ask to be dropped off at the junction of Collector's Hill and Sayle Road in Smith's Parish.

Smith's has a long and interesting history dating back to the early 17th century. Its home to the islands' largest and most diverse nature reserve, and a unique aquarium. Hikers and nature lovers will feel right at home here.

130

Stop 17, The Verdmont Museum, 441-236-7369, is close to the junction of Collector's Hill and Sayle Road. It's the finest historic house on the island. Thought to have been built Touring Devonshire in 1710 by ship owner John Dickinson, the house very much resembles an English country manor in the classic style, with four large chimneys above an unusual roof. Over the years a number of interesting people have called this their home.

The interior of the house is filled with the memorabilia of Bermudian history covering more than 250 years. The early family portraits were painted by John Green, an American loyalist refugee who fled to Bermuda from Philadelphia at the close of the War of Independence. Green married one of John Dickinson's granddaughters and soon became a prominent member of the islands' political community, being appointed a judge of the Court of the Vice Admiralty. The last private owner of the property was a somewhat eccentric old lady who lived out her lifetime, some 75 years, surrounded by memories. When she died, her family sold the old house to the Bermuda Historic Monuments Trust, now the Bermuda National Trust, who opened it to the public in 1956.

None of the furniture you see here belonged to the original owners of the house – only the family portraits by John Green. Even so, the furniture that does fill the house provides a cross-section of Bermudian and English styles over the 18th and 19th centuries. The handmade cedar staircase is unique; the newels have removable caps to accommodate candles. The upstairs nursery is filled with antique toys, and one has only to blink and look around to imagine small children at play dressed in the bright clothing of a bygone age.

Other items of interest at Verdmont include the two 19th century pianos and a fine china tea service, thought to have been a gift from the Emperor Napoleon to

President Madison. Unfortunately for Madison, the ship carrying it from France was set upon by privateers and the service was seized and ended up here in Bermuda. Verdmont is open every day (except Sunday) from April through October. Hours are from 9:30 am until 4:30 pm; 10 am until 4 pm, November through March. Admission is $5 for adults, $3 for senior citizens, and $1 for children and students with ID.

From Verdmont you can either catch the bus going east to St. George's or Grotto Bay, or you can hike down Collector's Hill to South Shore Road. If you walk, turn left on South Shore Road and go eastward for a mile to Spittal Pond, Stop 18 on your tour.

Spittal Pond, a 60-acre nature reserve, is Bermuda's showcase. Located along the shoreline overlooking the ocean, the park is interlaced with tiny paths and trails where, during the winter months, nature lovers can spend hours observing more than 25 species of waterfowl. In summer, the park is a profusion of flowers, plants and tropical trees. Be sure to check out Spanish Rock high on the bluff above the ocean.

The rock itself, found by the early settlers and carved with the date 1543 and other markings too indistinct to decipher, was removed from the spot now marked by a plaque to prevent further erosion. It is thought, though unconfirmed, that a Portuguese ship was wrecked on the island in 1543. The crew must have found a way off the island, however, because they were long gone by the time Sir George Somers arrived in 1609. You can see a plaster cast of the original carvings at the Museum of the Bermuda Historical Society in Hamilton. The Spittal Pond reserve is open daily from sunrise to sunset and admission is free.

Devil's Hole Aquarium

Stop 19 is Devil's Hole Aquarium, 441-293-2727. To reach it, you continue east along South Shore Road for a mile to Devil's Hole Hill and turn left to the Aquarium. Alternatively, take Knapton Hill to Harrington Sound Road and turn right. Both routes offer bus service; the distance is about the same. If you take a bus along South Shore Road you'll need to catch a number 1; if you go via Knapton Hill, take a number 3.

Devil's Hole Aquarium is the creation of a man named Trott, and it was Bermuda's first tourist attraction. Trott loved his fish and in 1830 he built a wall around his pond, a natural blue hole, to discourage people from fishing in it. This led to questions as to what he might be hiding behind his new wall. In order to allay any suspicions, he decided to allow people inside the wall to view the pond and, being an astute businessman, he charged admission.

Blue holes are formed when an underground, underwater cave collapses, leaving a deep pool. This one is fed by sea water from underground channels and caverns, thus it stays fresh and well-stocked with fish of all shapes and sizes. They say Devil's Hole contains more than 400 species of marine life, including giant grouper, turtles and sharks. You can fish in the pond if you like, but you can't really catch anything; the lines supplied by the staff are baited, but hook-less. Still, there's nothing quite like watching a four- or five foot shark nibbling at the end of your line; it might be the closest you'll ever get to catching one. Devil's Hole is open daily, May through October, from 9 am until 5 pm, and from 10 am until 3 pm, November through April. Admission is $5 for adults and $3 for children under 12.

To get to Stop 20, Flatts Village, go to the junction of Knapton Hill and take a number 3 bus westward (that's inbound toward Hamilton). A ride of about two miles brings you to the village.

Flatts Village is another neat little Bermudian community. A one-time haven for smugglers returning from the West Indies in the dead of night, it was also an occasional meeting place of the House of Assembly. Flatts is one of the oldest settlements on the islands and is very picturesque, located as it is on the shore of Harrington Sound. Today, the little town is a microcosm of Bermudian life, a collection of brightly painted cottages and houses, with tall palms and lots of flowering shrubs and plants.

Bermuda Aquarium and Zoo

Stop 21, The Bermuda Aquarium and Zoo, 441- 293-2727, www.bamz.org, is in Flatts Village. This is one of Bermuda's most popular attractions. It's an aquarium in the true sense of the word: educational as well as entertaining. The large glass tanks hold examples of most of the finny inhabitants of the reefs and oceans around Bermuda, including the predators: sharks, barracudas, even a moray eel. Then there are the small aquatic habitats that house the creatures we never hear about, but that are no less important to the underwater world they live in – tiny crabs, sea urchins and corals. The strange-looking sphere you see just outside is a replica of the bathysphere which Doctor Charles Beebe used for his famous half-mile-deep dive in 1934.

Beebe's Incredible Dive:

The highlight of Beebe's long career was, without doubt, his ocean dive. It was his insatiable desire to push the boundaries of the known world and his dedication to the study of sea life that led to the dive. In 1929 he built a marine laboratory and home in Bermuda on Nonesuch Island. There, with his second wife, Elswyth Thane, a novelist, he studied the sea life of the area. In 1930, in the true tradition of science fiction, he made his first descent into the ocean in a two-ton steel ball he called the bathysphere (a name derived from the Greek word bathys, meaning "deep"). In 1934, with Otis Barton, he made a dive of 3,028 feet, more than half a mile, and thus set a record for deep diving that wasn't broken until 1949.

Beebe was one of the 20th century's great adventurers, perhaps the last of a dying breed. Born in 1877, his career spanned more than 54 years and took him on explorations from the depths of the sea to the highest mountains, from Canada to South America, and from the steaming jungles of Borneo to the desolation of the Galapagos Islands. He received a bachelor of science degree at Columbia University in 1898, remained at Columbia for another year doing

Postgraduate work, and then, in 1899, the New York Zoological Society named him honorary curator of birds, and director of the Society's Department of Tropical Research. Beebe retired as director of the Department of Tropical Research in 1952, but he never stopped working. He continued his studies of jungle creatures at the New York Zoological Society's field station in Simla, in the mountains of Trinidad. He died in 1962 at the age of 85.

The Aquarium houses an exhibit that documents Beebe's epic dive. The aquarium itself contains a large collection of marine life, including reef fish, sharks and barracuda. The zoo has a fine collection of reptiles from around the world, and there's a children's discovery room where the kids can enjoy themselves working puzzles and coloring pictures. The Aquarium and Zoo are open daily from 9 am until 5 pm. Admission is $8 for adults; $4 for senior citizens and children under 12.

Touring Hamilton Parish

From Flatts Village, turn right on Wilkerson Avenue and follow the road for a short distance to Crystal Cave and Fantasy Cave, the first of two cave systems along the Harrington Sound Road. Crystal Cave was discovered in 1905 by two boys playing cricket.

Apparently, their ball disappeared down a hole and they went in after it. They found themselves in a vast underground cavern more than 120 feet deep, surrounded by rock formations of fantastic shapes and sizes and an underground lake.

Today, the entrance to the two caves the boys found is gone, replaced by a sloping path to a wooden bridge across the lake. If you've never been underground, you should try it here. The stalactites and stalagmites are accentuated by hidden lighting that glows among the rocks and shimmers across the still waters of the lake. 441-293-0640.

Before you leave the area, you might enjoy a visit to the Glass Blowing Studio. You'll find it at 16 Blue Hole Hill; 441- 293-2234. If you've never seen glass blowing done before, you're in for a treat. I'm not about to try to describe the process here; you have to see for yourself. Suffice it to say that it's one of the world's oldest arts, dating back more than 2,000 years.

Today, it's become a fine art, and the pieces made at the studio are among the best you're ever likely to see. The products are pure Bermudian: bowls, vases, plates and ornaments, all produced in the vibrant colors of the islands. Tour the studio, see how it's done, then take a piece home with you. The studio is open from 9 am until 5 pm, Monday through Saturday, and from 10 am until 5 pm on Sundays, January through August. September through December, it's open from 10 am until 4 pm. Prices range from about $12 for a small glass ornament to more than $100 for larger, more exotic pieces. Admission is free.

Go south from Crystal Caves along Harrington Sound Road for a short distance to Tom Moore's Tavern, Stop 24. It's not far and is an easy walk. The old tavern has its roots set firmly in Bermuda's history.

It was built by Thomas Trott in 1652. Trott called his new home Walsingham, after Robert Walsingham, a sailor on the Sea Venture, and for whom the nearby bay on Castle Harbour is named. Later it became the haunt of Irish poet, Tom Moore, who arrived on Bermuda in 1804. At that time the house was still owned by the descendants of Thomas Trott. Moore befriended them and paid frequent visits to the estate. In fact, he did much of his writing there. Today, the house is a popular restaurant, still surrounded by woods and gardens as it was when first built. It has lost little of its charm over the 350 years. The restaurant is open only for dinner. You'll have to make a reservation, 441-293- 8020, www.tommoores.com, and take either a taxi or a number 3 bus from Hamilton.

Leamington Caves, Stop 25, are just a little farther south along Harrington Sound Road. Again, it's just a short walk from Stop 24, so you can stroll in the sunshine and enjoy the view along the way.

Leamington Caves are smaller and less impressive than Cahow Lake. A grotto with lots of stalactites, stalagmites and other rock formations, it's still worth time out for a visit. One of the more interesting rock formations is an amber pillar the staff has named the Statue of Liberty. It's a little difficult to make the connection, but you can decide that for yourself.

If you'd like a bite to eat before you visit the cave, try the Plantation. Lunch will cost you $15 or so per person, but that entitles you to visit the caves for free. Otherwise the entrance fee is $4 for adults and $2 for children aged 4 to 12. The caves are open from 10 am until 4 pm, Monday through Saturday from mid-February through late November. They are closed December and January.

Continue south along Harrington Sound Road for about a mile to Tucker's Town, Stop 26. You can take a bus if you like, but the walk is quite pleasant if time allows. Daniel Tucker was one of the first governors of Bermuda. In 1616 he decided to move his home from St. George's to a new settlement on Castle Harbour. Work was begun on the new town. Some streets and small houses made it off the drawing board into reality, but eventually the project was abandoned.

Tucker's Town became a tiny fishing community and existed as such for 300 years until after the end of the First World War in 1918. Around that time a large tract of Tucker's Town was purchased for use as a country club and steamship dock. The result of that purchase is the Mid-Ocean Club and the Marriott Castle Harbour Hotel. Soon after the club was founded, its members started building homes in the surrounding area. Today, the community is the most affluent on the islands. Only club members are allowed to purchase property here and homes sell for upwards of $2 million.

Stop 27 is below the Mid-Ocean Golf Club clubhouse on the South Shore. Natural Arches is one of the most beautiful and, consequently, most photographed spots on the island. Its major attractions are the two natural stone arches carved by the action of the wind and surf over many thousands of years. Walk on down to the South Shore Road, where you'll find signs pointing the way to Castle Harbour and Natural Arches.

When you've finished at Natural Arches, continue eastward to Castle Island, Stop 28; you either have to walk or take a taxi. The walk is one of the most beautiful on the islands. You won't see many people along the way, but you will enjoy wonderful views and the fresh salt breeze. Castle Island is one of a group of islands located at the tip of the southern peninsula that bounds Castle Harbour. The islands were fortified by the first settlers soon after they landed on Bermuda in the early 17th century; hence the name Castle Harbour. Today,

138

the islands are a part of Bermuda's nature reserves, and you can go bird watching, hiking and picnicking along the way.

On the Water

Boating

Kayak Bermuda

I was wondering when some enterprising individual would realize what wonderful opportunities for sea kayaking are available on Bermuda; well, here we are at last.

Kayak Bermuda is the brainchild of Stephen "V" and Lexie McKey. At the time of writing, they don't have a full sea-going itinerary yet, but what they do have is something unique and extraordinarily appealing.

At the moment, they are specializing in short tours, 2½ to three hours, that anyone, experienced or not, can easily manage. They start with a practice paddle along Millionaire's Row at Tucker's Town and then continue on along the coral and limestone cliffs of the Castle Island Nature Reserve. There, you can observe the long tail birds and float over the coral reefs. After 35 to 45 minutes, you have the choice of relaxing on the beach or snorkeling, or you can continue kayaking another 20 to 25 minutes to reach some faster and more exciting paddling in the waves off the South Shore.

Then again, you might like to go on the evening tour, which will take you along the North Shore to observe the sunset. I've got to tell you, this sort of soft adventure really appeals to me. The company uses the safe "sit on top" kayaks that are stable and easy to use, even for first-timers; full instruction is included.

Tours depart at 9:30 am, 1:30 pm and 7 pm, June through September, from Ordnance Island & Penno's Wharf, St. George. The rate is $50 per person for all ages over eight years old. Children under 16 must paddle with an able adult. Payment is at the dock by cash or credit card. It's best to make a reservation; Contact Stephen or Virginia McKey at 441-737-7378.

Boat Rentals

"You can do it all with a Boston Whaler," at least that's what the brochure says, and they're "unsinkable," again according to the brochure. Seriously, though, if you love getting out and about on the water, you should consider renting one of these sturdy craft. They are available for rent at Somerset Bridge Water Sports, Robinson's Marina at Somerset Bridge, 441-234-0914. The boats travel at speeds up to 35 miles per hour, have center console steering, Bimini tops to provide shade from the midday sun, and you can take along optional snorkeling gear, fishing rods and tackle, and a cooler with ice, all for a nominal extra fee.

You can explore the coastline and its many secluded coves, tiny islands and beaches, or speed around the Great Sound. You can snorkel over a reef, off an island beach, or even over a shipwreck. If you want a secluded picnic, that's available too. You can even feed the fish over the shipwreck of the HMS Vixen.

All this is possible through map orientation and advice about route selection provided by Tony Roach, the owner of Water Sports. Tony's colored map highlights the best beaches, snorkeling spots, and where to find the best fishing, as well as convenient waterside restaurants. Never driven a boat before? Don't worry Tony's staff will show you how in just a few minutes; it's that easy.

You can rent a Boston Whaler at two hours for $60; four hours for $100; six hours for $140; and eight hours for $160. Gas is extra, costing about $15 for four hours. The boats will carry up to four adults (one adult equal's two children under 12 years old). Reservations are advised (no deposit is necessary) and you should plan to arrive about 30 minutes before you intend to depart. 441-234-0914.

Fishing

Nothing beats heading out to sea in the early morning just as the sun is peeping over the horizon, when the air is crisp and cool, with the breezes blowing gently in your face. And few things compare with the feeling one gets aboard a slowly trolling boat on a calm sea under a hot summer sun, a heavy rod between your knees, and a can of something cold in your hand.

The ultimate experience comes when you hook your first billfish and you find yourself involved in the fight of a lifetime as the fish does its utmost to tear rod and line from your aching fingers. In the distance, you see him hurl himself many feet into the air and drop down with a mighty splash as he tries to rid himself of the hook. And then you have him there at the side of the boat, exhausted, docile, deep blue back glistening in the sunlight, your first sailfish. And so it begins.

Photo Courtesy of the Bermuda Department of Tourism

You don't have to be a world-class angler to take advantage of what Bermuda has to offer. In fact, it's okay if you've never fished in your life. There are plenty of skilled guides on the islands willing to take you in hand and show you how it's done. A couple of hours of instruction, a fast boat or a calm, shallow-water flat, and you're in business, as surely hooked as any wahoo or amberjack – doomed to spend the rest of your days in search of "The Big One."

In recent years the numbers of fish on the reefs and in the shallow water within the reef line have declined. This situation has caused real concern and new government regulations have already done much to restore the dwindling finny population.

The quality of sport fishing in Bermuda is high year-round, but the prime season is between May and November. There are more species of fish in the waters off Bermuda than you're ever likely to catch, and you have several options as to how you might go about it. Of course, offshore fishing is the premier version of the sport in Bermuda, but there really is something for everyone.

You don't need to charter expensive deep-sea boats to enjoy a good day out. You can do it from a small rental boat all by yourself, from the beach, from a private dock or a hotel fishing pier. You're not likely to catch a trophy sailfish or marlin from the dock – you'll have to go to sea for that – but you will catch pompano, and perhaps even bonefish. The key is knowing where to fish.

The Catches

On the reef you'll find snapper, grouper, little tunny, Bermuda chub, and yellowtail, to mention only a few. In the deep waters beyond the reef are the great game fish. Besides the sailfish, the king of fish is perhaps the blue marlin, but they are few and far between. When you do find one, you're in for the experience of a lifetime. The "big blue" typically ranges in size from 100 to 200 pounds or more. Fish of three, four and five hundred pounds have been caught in more southern waters and stories of "the one that got away" tell of fish in excess of 1,000 pounds.

Bluefin tuna is another exciting blue-water catch. Fish weighing in at 100 pounds or more are not uncommon, and catches between 500 and 800 pounds have been recorded in the western Atlantic. Black fin and yellow fin tuna are smaller, but no less fun to catch. Other excellent deep water species include the kingfish, or king mackerel. They can be caught year-round, although peak seasons are the spring and summer.

Then there's dolphin. No, not Flipper; he's a mammal. This dolphin is a fish. Dolphin are usually found fairly close to the shoreline, weigh anywhere from five to 20 pounds, and are excellent to eat. Wahoo weigh 15 to 30 pounds and, in rare cases, as much as 60 pounds. They too make tasty dinners and are highly prized by sport fishermen. Wahoo are most often found lurking in the deep water off the edge of the reef. Amberjack is another prized sporting fish found most often in the cooler, deep waters just off the edge of the reef during the summer months, and closer to shore the rest of the year. Amberjack can run anywhere from 20 to 40 pounds.

Other species include white marlin, almaco jack, skipjack tuna and rainbow runner. Sharks, too, are common throughout the waters of the Bermudas and can be found in both shallow waters and deep. Makos, blues, hammerhead and tiger sharks abound. The truth is, however, that the fight usually lasts only as long as it takes for the shark's razor-like teeth to bite through the wire traces that hold him. Even so, you're sure to remember the battle for a long time. The wily barracuda is found in large numbers, in shallow or deep waters, and can often be seen swimming close to the surface in the clear waters over the reefs and sandy banks.

Barracuda range in size from a few pounds to about 15 or 20 pounds and, small though they might be, you're sure of a good fight if you can get one on the hook. Grouper is a tasty fish, often found swimming lazily, close to the bottom on the reefs all around Bermuda. Catches average 15 to 25 pounds, and fish of 30 to 45 pounds are not uncommon. Likewise the snapper. He, too, may be caught on the reefs throughout the islands. Most common are the red and gray variety.

Image Courtesy of Istockphoto

Licenses & Regulations

A fishing license is not required. You are not allowed to collect sea turtles, whales, porpoises and dolphins (the mammal), or corals of any type. Nor are you allowed to take the conch, helmet shells, bonnet shells, netted olive shells, Bermuda cone shells, scallops, the Atlantic pearl oyster, calico clams or West Indian tap shells.

No spear fishing is allowed within one mile of any shore; scuba gear may not be used to spear fish. A spear gun may not be used anywhere at any time. No more than two fish of any one species may be taken by spear fishing in any 24-hour period. Lobsters may only be taken from September 1st to March 31st, by licensed residents only.

Basic fishing information can be obtained from the Bermuda Department of Tourism, 441-292-0023, or from the Bermuda Game Fishing Association, PO Box HM 1306, Hamilton HM FX, Bermuda, 441-297-8093. The association is an advisory body representing the International Game Fish Association (IGFA) affiliated clubs in Bermuda, and is the caretaker for all official local records and world records held locally. 441-292-7131.

Visitors are encouraged to enter their catches in the annual Game Fishing Tournament (January 1st to December 31st) with the Bermuda Department of Tourism, Global House, 43 Church Street, Hamilton. No license is required and there is no entry fee. Awards are presented for top catches in 26 classes of fish found in local waters.

Qualifications for Awards

Twenty-six species of fish are recognized for competition purposes. The section below indicates these species and also advises maximum line test that may be used. Note: maximum line test does not apply to an entry for the Award of Merit. Awards.

The Award of Merit may be received by a visitor only. Entrants must use the official entry form. Any game fish caught on any test line can qualify. The Citation is made for an officially entered fish a) to a visitor catching a fish weighing at least 1½ times the test line used, and b) to a resident catching a fish weighing at least twice the test line used.

The Outstanding Angling Achievement Award is a handsome silver pin that may be won by catching one of four species of fish – greater amberjack, bonefish, yellow fin tuna, and wahoo – in a variety of ways: The Heaviest Fish in each Recognized Species caught by a visitor during any one year will win an award; the High Point Fish in each Recognized Species caught by a visitor in any one year will win an award.

Where to Find the Fish

Among the most popular spots for shore fishing at the western end of the islands are Great Sound, Little Sound, and many of the rocky beaches and inlets from Frank's Bay to the Royal Naval Dockyard. On the outside of the islands, the beaches from Long Bay southward around Daniel's Head, Ely's Harbour, and on to West Whale Bay seem to offer the best opportunities.

Going east, Castle Harbour and St. George's Harbour both offer good opportunities for a day's sport. The beaches off the extreme eastern end of the island around St. Catherine's Point, and the rocky shores around St. David's Head offer great possibilities too. You might also try the South Shore around John Smith's Bay and Devonshire Bay.

You can go fly-fishing for bonefish almost anywhere around the islands – in the tiny inlets, the sandy coves, and on the flats inside the reef. Bonefish are not very big. Most often they will weigh in around six to 15 pounds, with some growing to 20 pounds. Hook one, however, and you're in for a battle. Bonefish are known for fighting.

Reef & Deep-Sea Fishing

Reef fishing, or deep-sea fishing, is how you'll find "The Big One." The three major reef systems forming the tip of the extinct volcano that is Bermuda lie at varying distances from the islands. The first, the inner system, runs as close as a half-mile from the shore in some places and stretches outward almost five miles.

The second system, the Challenger Bank, lies 17 miles offshore; and the third, the Argus Bank, is more than 25 miles out. Trolling is the most popular method of fishing over the reefs, and catches of snapper, grouper, barracuda and amberjack are common. Just off the reef in deeper waters are wahoo, tuna, dolphin, sailfish and marlin.

Charter boats are available to take you out to the fishing grounds. They come in different sizes, from 28 feet to 55 feet, and are equipped with a variety of tackle with line-test weights from 20 to 130 pounds. Most boats are also fitted with all the modern gadgets for tracking the fish, including depth sounders, sonar, and radar.

Rental Equipment for Shore Fishing

Fishing tackle may be rented from any of the following outfits on a daily or weekly basis. You will be required to leave a deposit (usually about $30) in case of loss or damage of the equipment. Prices range from $10 per day to $50 or $60 per week.

Four Winds Fishing Tackle Ltd., 2 Woodlands, Road, Pembroke, HM 07 441292-7466

Mangrove Marina Ltd. End of Cambridge, Road, Mangrove Bay, Somerset 441-234-0914

Harbour Road Marina Newstead, Paget 441-236-6060

Pompano Beach Club & Waterports Centre, Pompano Beach Club, Southampton, 441-234-0222, extension 212

Sea Kettle Yacht Charters Ltd. (tackle comes with boat rental only), Sea Kettle, Paget 441-236-4863

Charter Boats for Deep-Sea & Reef Fishing

Some charter boats are available year-round, although the best fishing and charter deals are from May through November. All Bermudian charter boats are skippered by experienced guides and are equipped with fighting chairs and outriggers. All necessary tackle, bait, ship-to-shore telephones and lifesaving gear – rafts and life jackets – are included in the price of the charter. All you need to bring is lunch and refreshments.

All vessels have toilet facilities. Skippers operate under their own set of rules with regard to the fish that you might catch. You should, therefore, check out your prospective skipper's policy before you sign on. Does the boat retain all, or a percentage of the catch? Is there freedom of selection by the party renting the boat?

Rates & Hours

You can charter a boat by the half-day (four hours) or full day (eight hours) and rates vary according to the size of the boat and the reputation of its captain.

A four-hour trip will limit the grounds that may be fished. Parties of six persons are preferred. Charter rates differ from season to season, mainly due to the fluctuation of fuel prices, and the rate is often determined by the type of fishing you want to do, e.g. deep-sea, reef or bone fishing. All Bermudian charter

148

fishing boats are inspected annually by the Department of Marine & Ports Services and the Department of Fisheries, who then issue a license to operate. Check that current licenses are displayed when you board the boat.

Charters can be arranged privately or through one of the organizations listed below.

Charter Companies

The Bermuda Charter Fishing Boat Association, Box SB 145, Sandy's, Bermuda, SB BX, 441-292-6246

The Bermuda Sport Fishing Association, Creek View House, 8 Tulo Lane, Pembroke, Bermuda, HM 02, 441-295-2370.

The St. George's Game Fishing & Cruising Association, Box 107, St. George's, Bermuda, GE BX, 441-297-8093.

To book, call the individual charter captains direct or contact the member's association booking office. Independent Charter Fishermen have no stars at the beginning of their listings and must be called direct.

Outfitters

As with all things, captains come and go, and it's never really possible to stay up to date with the outfitters on Bermuda. All of the following were in business at the time of writing, but… well, you get the idea. So, be sure to call well in advance – at least three months.

Michael Baxter: 441-234-2963. Ellen B, 28-foot Down East; 14 rods, 4 to 50 pounds test; spinning to heavy troll; two depth sounders.

Alan Card: 441-234-0872. Challenger, 45-foot Flybridge Sportsfisherman; 26 rods; 12 to 130 pounds test; three fighting chairs; Loran; depth sounder; three outriggers and two downriggers.

Eddie Dawson, Sr.: 441-504-3474. Sea Scorpion III, 33-foot Young Brothers Flybridge; 10 rods; 12 to 80 pounds test; One fighting chair; two downriggers; Loran; radio depth sounder.

Allen DeSilva: 441-295-0835. Mako 4, 53-foot Jim Smith Sportsfisherman; 24 rods; fish finders; Loran; three fighting chairs; air-conditioning.

David DeSilva: Call the association booking office, 441-295-0835. Miranda, 47-foot Bermuda, custom built; 29 rods; 12 to 80 pounds test; three fighting chairs; fish recording machine; live bait well; two downriggers.

Eugene Dublin: Call the association booking office, 441-732-2207 or 441-292-2466. Princess, 31-foot Bertram; 10 rods; 12 to 80 pounds test; one trolling chair; Fish finders; two downriggers.

Willard "Joe" Kelly: _441-297-8093. Messaround, 40-foot Down East Sportsfisherman; 15 rods; 20 to 130 pounds test; fish finder; Loran; microcomputer; three fighting chairs; live well; outriggers and downriggers.

Robinson's Charter Boat Marina: 441-234-0709. Ladybird, 22-foot Cabin Cuddy Aquasport; mainly light tackle and spinning lines.

Allan Virgil: 441-238-2655. Lady Gina, 35-foot Bertram Sportsfisherman; selection of rods and reels; 30 to 130 pounds test; three downriggers; center rigger; live bait well; fighting chair; Loran; color depth and fish finder.

Blake West: _441-293-0813. Troubadour, 42-foot Double Ender; nine rods; 12 to 80 pounds test; depth sounder; outriggers and downriggers.

John Whiting & Miles Mayall: 441-534-8590. Atlantic Spray, 40-foot custom-built Sportsfisherman; 12 custom-built rods; 12 to 130 pounds test; depth sounder.

Russell Young: 441-234-1832. Sea Wolfe, 43-foot Torres custom-built Sportsfisherman; selection of rods; 20 to 130 pounds test; downriggers and outriggers; three fighting chairs; live well; refrigerated fish hold; color fish finder; Loran; VHF; Epirb; air-conditioned lounge.

Diving

Bermuda offers excellent diving. There are a number of qualified dive operators on the islands, all with expert knowledge of the waters and willing to take you on scheduled dives, or to locations of your own choosing. Unless you have an extensive diving background, it's probably best to take advantage of their knowledge, especially if you want to look for shipwrecks. For the most part, the waters off Bermuda are very clear, shallow and offer an abundance of coral reefs and underwater gardens for you to enjoy and explore, as well as more than 300 known shipwrecks, modern and ancient.

Dangerous Denizens of the Deep

As always, there are dangers, natural and manmade, that you should take into consideration when stepping out of your natural environment. The following are some that you should be particularly wary of:

Sharks. The most feared predator of the deep, with a bad and, for the most part, undeserved reputation. Peter Benchley's graphic movie, Jaws, based upon a fantasy of his own, has done much to enhance our natural fear of the shark. The truth is, the shark, like every other life-form on earth except man, kills only when hungry and rarely will it attack a human. Shark attacks are rare, especially in Bermuda. They say you have more chance of being struck by lightning, twice, than of being attacked by a shark. Even so, especially if you are unable to identify them, it's best that you steer clear of all sharks you might see.

Moray eels are nocturnal creatures and like very much to be left alone inside their chosen lair. There are a few that have become used to humans and their handouts, but most morays can, if disturbed or threatened, give you a very nasty bite. Stay at a respectful distance.

151

Barracuda. Not really dangerous, just scary-looking, especially their rather frightening, ever-present grin. The sleek, silver tiger of the ocean is curious, however, and will often follow you around. If someone is feeding the local reef fish (which they shouldn't), be on the lookout for something bigger. A barracuda after his share of the pie attacks like lightning and, although he's only after a handout, it might be a hand he takes.

Reef fish, such as the Black Hamlet, tend to be curious and, while they're not dangerous, you might find them nipping at your fingers, toes and hair.

Rays, on the whole, are not dangerous. Tread on a stingray buried in the sand, however, and you're probably in for a trip to the local hospital. The ray's first reaction is self-preservation, and its natural instinct is to lash out with that murderous tail. Unless threatened or trodden on, rays are pretty much harmless and are fascinating to observe as they flap over the sandy bottom. Watch where you put your feet.

Scorpion fish can often be found lying in wait on coral heads or close to the ocean floor. The thick spines on its back can inflict a nasty sting, but this will happen only if you startle one.

Sea urchins are the spiky little black balls that lie on the sandy ocean floor or in the nooks and crannies of coral heads in shallow water. Step on one with your bare feet at your peril. The spines are brittle, often barbed, and will give you a very nasty and painful experience. Fortunately, they are usually easy to see and can be avoided. Keep a sharp look out and don't touch.

The stonefish, often hard to see due to excellent camouflage, can also give a nasty sting.

Jellyfish, transparent and often difficult to see, are mostly harmless. There are, however, some that are not and it's best if you avoid them all.

Coral is often sharp and can become dislodged in cuts and abrasions, which will leave you in pain for a couple of days. Fire coral can be a problem, but only if you're foolish enough to handle it. Try not to touch coral at all. Not only can it be dangerous, it's a delicate, living organism that can easily be damaged.

If you do happen to get stung by coral, jellyfish, or urchin, you can treat the sting first with vinegar, which will neutralize the stinging cells. You should then get ointment from the local drugstore to ease the pain.

Wreck Diving

There are said to be more than 300 shipwrecks in the waters off Bermuda. Some of these, especially those that allow access to their interiors, can be dangerous if you aren't familiar with them or don't know what you're doing. Even experienced divers should not go alone into unknown wrecks. There are plenty of guides and dive operators around who have years of experience with each wreck and know what to avoid; it's best to hire one when you embark upon your journey into the dark unknown. Many wrecks are infested with fire coral and others are home to moray eels.

Photo Courtesy of Istockphoto

153

Do not do this alone, or without an experienced. It's really not that dangerous out there if you take reasonable precautions and stay alert. You'll only get into trouble if you do something you shouldn't, are neglectful, or fail to take note of the instructions you'll receive from your guide. So be careful and never dive alone.

Where & When

While the majority of dive operators conduct trips throughout most of the year, May through October offers the best water for diving and snorkeling. It's clear, warm and quiet. No prior certification for scuba diving is necessary; you can learn when you get there. The costs range from $95 for a one tank dive to $135 for two tanks. Lessons start at around $175 for novices, and you can be out on the reef the same afternoon. Most of the larger resort hotels offer some sort of diving package, including three-hour courses of instruction for beginners. These cost about $195, and that includes the use of equipment.

Just about any underwater experience you fancy is available off Bermuda's beach reefs. The coral is honeycombed with ledges, caves and caverns, and the depth varies from just a few feet to more than a thousand beyond the drop-offs. The marine life is abundant, colorful and curious, and you can spend endless hours with just a snorkel, mask and fins, never leaving the shallows.

Shipwrecks lie in waters that vary in depth from a few feet below the surface to more than 100 feet. Of these, only 40 are in good enough condition to offer an interesting dive. The best wrecks are described in this chapter. Most of the operators know where the wrecks are and are knowledgeable about the water and conditions prevailing at each site. It is highly recommended that you go with an experienced guide.

Helmet Diving

Hartley's Underwater Wonderland, 866-836-3989 or 441-234-3535, at Somerset Bridge, is one of Bermuda's most unusual adventures. Reminiscent of the undersea walk depicted in the movie 20,000 Leagues under the Sea, the three-hour cruise is sure to be one of the highlights of any vacation. You'll leave Somerset Bridge aboard a 50-foot diesel-powered vessel complete with hot shower. Captain Bronson Hartley and a crew of two, and head out to the reef. There, you'll don your helmet – yes, you can keep your glasses on and you won't even get your head wet – and descend a ladder to the ocean floor, a depth of 10 to 15 feet.

You walk the sandy bottom for 30 minutes or so and see the colorful coral formations and hundreds of multicolored fish waiting for handouts. No matter what your age, from five to 85, if you can negotiate the ladder, you can enjoy the wonders of the undersea world, and you don't even have to be able to swim.

The entire experience is like a walk in a garden. Is it safe? You bet.

Bronson Hartley is highly experienced. As a young man, he dove with Charles Beebe (see pages 112). Hartley's Reef Safari, 441-234-3535, www.hartleybermuda.com. The cost of a dive is $95; just bring your swimsuit and a towel. Hot chocolate is provided when the water temperature is below 80°. Wetsuits are available during the winter months.

The Shipwrecks

Bermuda's reefs have, over the past 400 years or so, claimed hundreds of ships, and there's no doubt that they will continue to do so.

The 33 wrecks listed here are the best-known and offer the most interesting dives. Once again, regardless of experience, you should never dive the wrecks, much less enter them, without an experienced guide. You'll find a list of operators with the required experience at the end of this chapter. Each wreck is listed by name.

The **Beaumaris Castle** lies in 25 feet of water on the outer edge of the reef some two miles east of St. Catherine's Point. She was an English steel-hulled sailing ship built in Glasgow, Scotland, in 1864. Beaumaris Castle was 202 feet long, 36 feet across the beam, and displaced just over 1,000 tons.

She ran aground carrying a cargo of jute and linseed oil on April 24th, 1873, while en route from Calcutta, India, to New York. Within hours, a number of small boats had rushed to offer assistance. Unfortunately, they could do little for the stricken ship other than rescue the crew and salvage a little of her cargo. Coincidentally, units of the Coast Wrecking Company of New York were, at the same time, operating in Bermudian waters, and they were called in to refloat the ship.

The weather, however, held up operations until early June, when powerful pumps were installed in the ship's holds. The salvage operations were abandoned when a crew member, overcome by gasses while trying to clear a clogged pump, died, and three others, including the captain, were also overcome and had to be taken ashore. Slowly, over the years, the wreck deteriorated to her present condition, a scattering of bits and pieces on the northern side of Mill's Breakers.

The **Blanch King** was an American schooner built in Maine in 1887. Today, she lies in 35 feet of water on the reef some three miles east of Ely's Harbour. The ship, a fourmasted, two-decker, was 192 feet long, 42 feet across the beam, and displaced 1,156 tons. On December 2nd, 1920, she was heading from Norfolk, Virginia, to Bermuda with a cargo of coal. She hit the reef and sank; all eight crew members managed to get off safely. The main portion of the wreckage includes some machinery and the center board box that housed a retractable keel. Bits and pieces of cable, rigging and fixtures lie scattered over the reef.

The **Caesar** was an English wooden sailing ship built in Durham, England, 1814. On July 3rd, 1818, Caesar was en route from England to Baltimore with a cargo of grindstones, medicine, glassware, clock parts and lead oxide when she fouled the reef about three miles west of Ely's Harbour and sank. Today she lies in pieces in 35 feet of water, not far from the wreck of the Blanch King. She's been thoroughly worked over since her discovery, but you can still see a part of her cargo of grinding wheels, and you might, if you're lucky, find an old bottle or two.

The **Caraquet** was an English mail packet built at the Harland & Wolfe shipyard in Belfast, Ireland, in 1894. On June 25th, 1923, while on the way from St. John to Halifax, rough seas, fog and abnormally strong currents pushed her off course and she ended up on the rocks 10 miles north of Hamilton. All of her crew and passengers made it safely off the ship before she sank in 45 feet of water, where she lies today. The massive wreck, scattered over a wide area, is a great dive. Enormous boilers, a great anchor, winches, capstans, machinery, plates, beams and all sorts of other bits and pieces provide a mighty backdrop for underwater photographers and are great for explorers.

H.M.S. Cerberus, a 32-gun English Navy ship-of-the-line built in 1779, was lost after hitting the rocks while leaving Castle Harbour sometime early in 1783. The crew tried valiantly to save the sinking ship. They threw its guns and shot overboard, cut its masts and rigging adrift, but all to no avail and, eventually, they were ordered to abandon ship. In the days that followed, further efforts were made to salvage the guns and gun carriages, and some were eventually brought ashore. Cerberus was 126 feet long, 36 feet across the beam, and displaced a little more than 700 tons. She lies just off King's Island, to the south of Castle Harbour.

The **Colonel William Ball** was a magnificent luxury yacht built in 1929 and typical of those extravagant times. Originally named Sialia, and then Egeria, she was 120 feet long with a 23-foot beam, and displaced 291 tons. In 1941 she was acquired by the U.S. Army Transportation Corps and renamed Colonel William Ball; she ran aground in bad weather on Mill's Breakers, two miles east of St. Catherine's Point. Today she lies in about 20 feet of water close to the wreck of the Beaumaris Castle.

The **Constellation** was made famous as the subject of the movie The Deep, based upon a novel by Peter Benchley. She was a four-masted sailing ship built in Maine in 1918. From the time of her launching, she enjoyed a somewhat off-beat career. At one time, plans were afoot to turn her into a floating school and, with that in mind, she was completely refitted and provided with all the modern conveniences, including electricity and refrigeration. Alas, those plans came to naught. At the outbreak of the Second World War, she was converted yet again, this time as a freighter.

In 1942, she set sail from New York with a cargo of Scotch whiskey, cement, and drugs; her destination was La Guira, Venezuela. She ran into difficulties in high seas soon after leaving New York and began to take on water. Her steamdriven pumps broke down and what little the crew could do with the hand pumps was not enough. Her captain decided to head for Bermuda to make repairs.

On July 30th, 1942, in calm seas and while waiting for a pilot to guide her into port, she was taken by strong currents and driven hard onto the rocks five miles northwest of the entrance to Great Sound; she was a total loss. It's laughable that the U.S. Navy was able to salvage only a select amount of Constellation's cargo.

Seven hundred cases of Scotch whiskey were retrieved; the cement and the drugs remained in the wreck. And it was those drugs that were the inspiration for Peter Benchley's novel. Today, Constellation lies where she sank all those years ago, on a sandy bottom in about 30 feet of water. She has not suffered the years underwater very well.

Her remains are strewn over a wide area and her cargo of cement is easily seen – a huge pile of hardened bags on the sandy bottom. There are still quite a few pieces of cargo waiting to be found, including some of the drugs.

The **Cristobal Colon** was a Spanish luxury liner built in 1923. She was 500 feet long, 61 foot in the beam, and displaced almost 11,000 tons. She was one of the finest and most luxurious passenger ships of her time. On October 25th, 1936, the vessel was heading from Cardiff, Wales, to Vera Cruz, Mexico with 160 crew members aboard, but no passengers. Her captain, Cresencia Navarro Delgardo, decided to swing by Bermuda in order to check the instruments. He was steaming at 15 knots some eight miles north of the island and to the east of North Rock when he sighted a light, which he believed to be the lighthouse at St. David's.

A short while later he saw a closer blinking light, which he thought must be the North Rock Beacon; it wasn't. The beacon had been out of service for more than a week, and bad weather had prevented repairs. Delgardo altered course away from what he thought was the beacon and ran hard onto North Rock itself.

The crew all managed to make it safely ashore, but their troubles weren't ended. At that time, the Spanish Civil War was still raging and many believed the

Cristobal Colon was on her way to Mexico to pick up weapons for the Spanish government. Be that as it may, the Spanish Government seemed in no hurry for the return of the stranded crew and, believing their own government would have to pick up the tab for the crew's keep, the Bermudians put them to work.

Finally, however, they embarked for Spain on Christmas Eve, 1936. Legend has it that, upon their return, General Franco had them all executed. For a number of years the wreck sat high in the water on the rocks eight miles from the islands. Her position made salvage an easy task. Her furniture, fittings, equipment, and art work were all taken from the ship. Many of the best pieces were stolen by looters who arrived under cover of darkness in fleets of motley boats.

Even today, Bermudian homes are adorned with bits and pieces from the wreck. Of the hundreds of islanders who plundered the great ship, only 13 were caught and brought to trial; of those, 12 were convicted. High in the water and intact as she was, the Cristobal Colon was a hazard to other shipping. Not that they would run into her. She looked for all the world like she was still under way. In 1937, the captain of Iristo, a Norwegian ship, spotted the wreck and, believing her to be negotiating the channel, he decided to follow her in. Within minutes, he, too had run afoul of North Rock.

This brought some action. The Colon was stripped of her masts and funnels in an effort to warn other ships away. When war broke out in Europe the once-proud ocean liner became a target for U.S. Air Force bombers. Slowly but surely she was blown apart, reduced to the waterline, and then to rubble spread over a wide area on the ocean floor.

Today, she is still the largest shipwreck in Bermuda. She lies in shallow water on both sides of the reef that caused her demise. She is, perhaps, one of the most interesting underwater sites in the islands – a photographer's dream come true. Her eight massive boilers, machinery, winches, and propellers can be seen at various depths from 15 feet to more than 70 feet.

The Curlew left Halifax on March 14th, 1856, bound for Bermuda and St. Thomas. She was a 182-foot, three-masted English sailing steamer, 22 feet across the beam and had a displacement of 528 tons. By the early morning hours of March 17th she was off the northern coast of Bermuda fighting heavy seas. Despite all efforts, she ran aground on the reef eight miles north of St. Catherine's Point, about a mile west of the Cristobal Colon.

The captain gave orders for the crew to abandon ship, but the seas were heavy and the weather poor; three of her four lifeboats were lost in the launching. The fourth was successfully put to sea and made it safely ashore where its crew raised the alarm.

Two Navy ships were immediately dispatched to the Curlew's aid and the rest of her crew, now clinging to the rigging for dear life, were taken off the ship. Today, there's not much left to see here. A victim of the incessant pounding of the breakers, she lies scattered on the reef in 35 feet of water a mile west of North Rock.

The **Darlington,** while en route from New Orleans to Bremen in Germany, was lost on the rocks of the Western Reef six miles west of Ely's Harbour on February 22, 1886. The Darlington was a fairly new ship, built at the massive Swan & Hunter shipyard in Newcastle, England, in 1881. She was a steamer, 285 feet long, 36 feet across the beam, and displaced 1,990 tons. On her last voyage she was carrying a cargo of cotton and grain.

Her loss was blamed on her captain, Richard Ward. It seems he failed to post a lookout while sailing in unfamiliar waters. Her crew of 28 officers and men were all rescued. The Darlington lies on her port side, collapsed flat, but still fairly intact. She's been under 15 to 30 feet of water now for more than 100 years.

The **Eagle** was wrecked on the breakers northeast of North Rock and eight miles north of St. Catherine's Point on January 12th, 1659. She was an English ship owned by the Virginia Company and was sailing from England to Jamestown when she struck the rocks. Her passengers and crew all made it safely ashore. The wreck was discovered, quite by accident, in 1956 when the yacht, Elda, was wrecked on the same site. Today, what little is left of the Eagle lies 35 feet beneath the surface a little more than a mile east of the Cristobal Colon.

The Hermes was taking a cargo of used goods and gifts to the poor in the Cape Verde Islands when she broke down in Bermudian waters. For a long time she lay abandoned, too expensive to repair. Eventually the government gave her to the Bermuda Divers Association, who stripped her and then, in 1984, sank her a mile offshore, south of Horseshoe Bay.

The Hermes was built in Pennsylvania in 1943. She was a 165-foot freighter and displaced 254 tons. Today, she lies upright and completely intact on the ocean bottom in about 80 feet of water. She is, without doubt, the most photogenic wreck in the islands. Divers can explore the wreck, inside and out. All hatches were removed prior to sinking, allowing unobstructed access to the cargo hold, engine room, pilot house and galley. She's one of the most popular shipwreck sites in Bermuda.

The Iristo, mentioned earlier, was a Norwegian-owned steamer built in 1918 in Ohio. She was 251 feet long, almost 44 feet across the beam, and displaced more than 1,820 tons. Between the time of her construction and her passing, she changed owners and names several times, finally becoming the Iristo and the property of Hans F. Grann in 1936. In March, 1937, she was en route from St. John's in Newfoundland to Bermuda with a cargo of flour, gasoline, a fire engine and a steam roller when her captain spotted the wreck of the Cristobal Colon.

Thinking the wreck was on her way through the channel into Bermuda, Captain Christian Stephenson decided to follow the Colon into port. He did, in fact, follow her onto the reef. Iristo was pulled off the reef that same afternoon by a seagoing tug out of St. George's.

The damage to her hull was extensive and she sank the next day about a mile east of North Rock and seven miles north of St. Catherine's Point. Captain Stephenson was charged with negligence. Iristo now lies in 50 feet of water. Her bow and stern sections are intact and, with her anchors, propeller, boilers and machinery, provides divers with a great underwater experience and photographic opportunities.

The **Kate** was an English, steel-hulled steamer en route from Galveston to La Havre, France, when she sank just a few hundred yards south of John Smith's Bay on December 10th, 1878. The ship, built in Whitby, England, in 1874, was some 200 feet long and displaced more than 1,400 tons. She was carrying a cargo of cotton when she went down. Her loss, so it seems, was caused by a series of disastrous events that took place over several days.

First, she struck an uncharted reef 22 miles northwest of the islands on November 30th. Then she hit Long Bar and sprang her plates. In an unsuccessful attempt to save her, she was taken under tow, but had to be grounded when she started to sink. Then, on December 10th, the weather turned nasty and the ship was blown off the sandy bottom into deeper water, where she became completely submerged. The bulk of the wreck – her boilers, engine, propeller shaft and other machinery – lie in about 45 feet of water.

The **King** was a diesel-powered Navy tugboat built in 1941. Toward the end of her days, she was converted into a treasure salvage boat and then into a dive boat owned by Gary Lamb. Lamb donated the old boat as a potential dive site. In 1984, she was sunk a half-mile off the South Shore by South Side Scuba, where she lies intact in 65 feet of water. The wreck offers divers all sorts of exciting underwater opportunities. The pilot house and galley, now home to colorful marine life, are easily accessible, and there are lots of sights for underwater photographers.

The **Lartington** left Savannah, Georgia, on December 8th, 1879, bound for Revel in Russia with a cargo of 4,000 bales of cotton. By the morning of December 10th, she was off the northwest coast of Bermuda fighting a gale and heavy seas. At eight o'clock that morning, she was struck by a massive wave that cracked her hull and she began to take on water.

For the rest of the day the ship's pumps labored to keep her afloat. By the morning of the 12th her captain could see that they were fighting a losing battle and decided to head for Bermuda. She never made it. Lartington ran aground on the rocks five miles northwest of the Royal Naval Dockyard on the morning of the 14th of December. Today, the old ship lies scattered across the sea bottom, close to the wreck of Constellation, in 15 to 30 feet of water. Her bow is still intact and divers can explore parts of her stern section, her boilers and propeller.

L'Herminie was a 60-gun wooden-hulled French frigate, 300 feet long, built and launched in 1824. She was a part of a squadron of warships sent to Mexican waters in 1837 to enforce French claims in the area.

Unfortunately, a fourth of her crew came down with yellow fever and she was recalled to France. By December 3rd, 1838, she was fighting heavy seas and bad weather. Her captain, Commodore Bazoch, decided to seek shelter in Bermuda.

She struck a reef and ran aground four miles west of Daniel's Head. Fortunately, her crew, almost 500 officers and men, were all taken safely ashore by local boats that came swiftly to assist. L'Herminie lies in 30 to 35 feet of water. All that's left of the old wooden ship are a couple of her guns, some cannon balls, and a large anchor. Even so, she makes a splendid dive site, and the two guns offer a neat photographic opportunity.

The **Madiana** was a Canadian-owned steel-hulled passenger steamship built in Scotland in 1877. She was 345 feet long, 39 feet across the beam, and displaced a little more than 3,000 tons. She was launched as the Balmoral Castle, changed owners and names in 1882, was sold again just before the turn of the century and reverted back to her original name; then was purchased by the Quebec Steamship Company and renamed Madiana.

She was en route from New York to the West Indies when, on February 10th, 1903, negotiating the channel into Hamilton Harbour, she ran onto the reef just northwest of North Rock, 10 miles north of the Royal Naval Dockyard. The crew fired distress rockets and tugs were sent to help.

Unfortunately, bad weather and heavy seas made it impossible for them to get closer than a mile from the ship. Lifeboats were launched and the passengers and crew hauled through raging seas to the relative safety of awaiting boats. Today, the wreck lies on the bottom where she went down, a mile west of the wreck of Caraquet, in about 25 feet of water.

The Marie Celeste. There's a name to conjure with. Marie Celeste was a Confederate Civil War blockade runner and, by all accounts, was a very successful one. Records prove that she made at least five successful trips past the Federal blockade squadrons. She was a steam-driven side-wheeler and one of the swiftest ships in her class.

She left port in Bermuda on September 14th, 1864, bound for Wilmington, North Carolina, with a cargo of meat, rifles and ammunition. She made swiftly through the channel toward the open sea, but hadn't been under way long when the first officer informed the pilot, a Bermudian by the name of John Virgin, that he could see breakers ahead. Virgin informed him that he knew "every rock here as well as I know my own house." The words were barely out of his mouth when the ship smashed into the reef. She went down, bow first, in a matter of minutes.

The ship's cook went down with her. He had gone down to his cabin to fetch some personal belongings and never made it back. Marie Celeste lies in 50 feet of water just 600 yards off the south coast. Although the wreck has deteriorated over the years, it still offers a great many excellent underwater photographic opportunities. Parts of the wheelhouse are still discernible. The bow section, engine and the hubs of her paddle wheels, especially the one on her starboard side which is standing upright, are all visible.

The **Minnie Breslauer** was an English steamer on her maiden voyage when she was lost off the coast of Bermuda on January 1st, 1873. She was en route from Malaga to New York with a cargo of fruit, wine and lead when she hit the reef. Rescuers managed to pull the ship off the rocks and she headed to St. George's for repairs. Unfortunately, she was too severely damaged and went down a mile off the coast, south of Horseshoe Bay, where she lies in some 60 feet of water. She has been pretty well destroyed by more than 100 years under water, but parts of her stern section are still discernible, as are her boiler and propeller.

The **Montana** was an English blockade runner operating between London and the southern ports of the Confederacy. She was a sleek, swift, side-wheeler paddle steamer, 236 feet long, 25 feet across the beam and displaced 750 tons.

Montana was powered by twin 260 horsepower engines that could push her at more than 15 knots. She operated covertly under a number of names other than Montana. Paramount, Nola, Gloria are but a few. On December 30th, 1863, she was heading from London to Wilmington and making for port in Bermuda to take on coal when she ran aground on the reef six miles northwest of the Royal Naval Dockyard.

Montana is in 30 feet of water, close to the wreck of Lartington, and within swimming distance of the wreck of Constellation. Her bow section is still fairly intact. The fantailed stern section lies a short distance from the main part of the wreck and is also recognizable. Her engines and paddle wheels lie near the center of the site, which is great for underwater photography.

The **North Carolina** was another steel-hulled, threemasted English vessel en route from Bermuda to Liverpool on January 1st, 1880. She was carrying a cargo of cotton when she ran onto the reef seven miles or so west of Ely's Harbour. She was 205 feet long and displaced 533 tons. Some attempts were made to salvage the ship, but the efforts failed and she went down. North Carolina lies in 20 to 50 feet of water. Her bow and stern sections remain intact and provide wonderful underwater photographic opportunities.

The **Pelinaion** was a Greek freighter built in Glasgow, Scotland, in 1907. She was 386 feet long, almost 50 feet across the beam, and displaced almost 4,300 tons. Originally built for the Hill Steam Ship Company, she changed hands and names several times before coming under Greek ownership. In 1936 she was renamed Pelinaion; it was the name she died with.

She was headed from Takiradi, in West Africa, for Baltimore with a cargo of iron ore when, on December 22nd, 1939, she hit the reef a mile south of St. David's Head. The lighthouse was under blackout because of the war in Europe. Pelinaion sits off St. David's head in 20 to 65 feet of water, fairly well strewn across the reef. Photographers should bring their cameras. The bow section sits only 20 feet below the surface, a huge engine sits upright and makes a fantastic photographic backdrop, while all around, her deck machinery, anchor and propeller provide more interesting views. 148 Diving Shipwrecks 149

The **Pollockshields** was built in Hamburg in 1890. She was a steamer, originally named Herodot, 323 feet long, 40 feet across the beam, displaced 2,744 tons, and carried a crew of 37. At the outbreak of the First World War, she became a German supply ship and was on the way from New York to the Azores when she was overtaken and captured by the British warship Argonaut.

The British government renamed her and set her to work. On September 7th, 1915, she was off Elbow Beach in heavy fog with a cargo of munitions. She struck the reef there within sight of the beach. The ship's captain, Earnest Boothe, was lost while the crew were taking to the boats, swept overboard in heavy seas. The rest of the crew made it safely ashore.

The wreck of Pollockshields was quite an event for the guests at the Elbow Beach Hotel, then the South Shore Hotel. They all turned out to watch the drama. The wreck lies scattered in shallow water just off Elbow Beach and can easily be reached by swimmers and snorkelers. Great care should be exercised, however, as the surge of the breakers and the undertow can be dangerous, especially on windy days. The site is a good one for divers. There's lots to see and explore, including live shells and other ammunition.

The **Ramona** was a large Canadian yacht that went down on December 2nd, 1967. The 120-foot steel-hulled yacht ran aground on the reef at eight o'clock in the evening. Her distress signals went unnoticed and the crew of 10 abandoned ship.

The wreck was spotted early the following morning and rescuers rushed to the site. Unfortunately, it was too late for some members of the crew. Only five of them survived. The wreck of Ramona was raised some time later, in the hopes that she could be repaired, but the damage was too extensive and the work too costly, so she was stripped and taken to a site off the north shore of the Royal Naval Dockyard and sunk in 60 feet of water.

The **San Antonio** was a Portuguese merchant ship headed from Cartegena to Cadiz on September 12th, 1621, with a cargo of hides, indigo, sarsaparilla, and tobacco, as well as 5,000 pounds of gold and silver, when she ran onto the western reef about eight miles from Ely's Harbour. She displaced some 300 tons and was armed with 12 cannons.

The story of the wreck tells of 120 survivors making it safely ashore, only to fall prey to wreckers on Bermuda who tortured them and made them give up the secret of the ship's treasure. Most of the gold and silver was recovered by the wreckers under the supervision of Bermuda's Governor Butler. The ship's anchors and most of her guns were also retrieved.

The wreck was found in 20 feet of water in 1960. A cannon was discovered, along with odds and ends of pottery, some coins, a gold chain and a jeweled ring.

Today, there's little left of the wreck for divers to see, and no treasure at all.

The **San Pedro** was also on her way from Cartegena to Cadiz loaded with treasure and other goodies. The year was 1596 and the 350-ton Spanish ship was lost on the reef eight miles north of the Royal Naval Dockyard. She was discovered by Teddy Tucker in 1951 when he spotted some cannon lying in 30 feet of water. He raised the cannon and sold them to the Bermudian government, but it wasn't until five years later that Tucker was able to work the site extensively.

The San Pedro became the first major modern treasure site. Tucker's first find was a 32-ounce gold bar, two smaller gold bars, and an emerald-studded gold cross. By the time the salvage work was finished, countless treasures and artifacts had been recovered.

Much of what Tucker discovered was put on display at the Aquarium Museum. Unfortunately, the famous emerald cross was stolen from its display case; a plastic replica was left in its place. The cross is still missing. Today, there is no treasure and no artifacts for you to discover. All that's left of the ancient Spanish ship are a few timbers and some ballast lying in 15 to 30 feet of water.

On a personal note: some few years ago, I was privileged to spend an evening with Teddy Tucker. What an interesting character he is. Oh, and by the way, he introduced me to his personal cache of rum, which also has a fine character.

The **Sea Venture**. No list of Bermudian shipwrecks would be complete without an account of the one that started it all. The remains of the ship that brought Sir John Somers to the islands in 1609 were discovered in 1958 as a result of a carefully planned search by Edmund Dowding. Dowding's research indicated the vessel must lie somewhere within an area to the east of

St. David's Head, known as Sea Venture Shoal. He began his search in June and found the wreck in October, lying in 30 feet of water. A representative of the Smithsonian was called in, along with local expert, 150 Diving Teddy Tucker, and the wreck was positively identified as that of the Sea Venture.

The **Taunton** was a Norwegian, steam-driven freighter built in Copenhagen in 1902. She was some 230 feet long, 33 feet across the beam, and displaced more than 1,300 tons. She was bound from Norfolk, Virginia to St. George on November 24th, 1920, with a cargo of coal, when she slammed into the reef eight miles north of St. Catherine's Point.

What's left of Taunton lies close to the surface and several other wrecks, including Eagle, in 20 feet of water. Although the ship is fairly well broken up and scattered across the reef, her engine and boilers offer spectacular backdrops for underwater photography, and the site is great fun to explore.

The **Virginia Merchant** was lost on March 26th, 1661. She had put into Castle Harbour to pick up supplies and fresh water on her way from Plymouth, England to Jamestown. She had just set sail again with 179 passengers when she ran aground on the rocks 250 yards off the South Shore at Sonesta Beach. All but 10 of her passengers and crew were lost.

She was discovered in shallow waters on the breakers. All that's left are the anchor, some pieces of wood, and a small pile of ballast.

H.M.S. Vixen was a three-masted, steam-driven British gunboat, built and launched in England at Deptford in 1867. She was a strange craft. Her iron hull was sheathed with teak in an experimental effort to overcome the problems the new ironclad ships were having with marine organisms. She was an inside-out ironclad, and a marine disaster.

Far from curing the problems, the teak sheathing added to them. It produced drag and added to her overall weight, thus making her the Royal Navy's slowest ironclad and rendering her nine-foot ram useless. The ship was basically unseaworthy, though she was the Royal Navy's first twin-screwed vessel. She was withdrawn from service in 1887 and taken to Bermuda as a part of the islands' coastal defense system. In 1896 she was stripped of her engines and fittings and scuttled in a narrow channel off Daniel's Head to block the way against possible attacks against the Royal Naval Dockyard.

The old ship lies just where the Royal Naval engineers left her. Her bow sticks up above the surface and her hull is still pretty much intact. She has been classified as a protected wreck, which means you'll need a permit to scuba dive over the wreck, though you won't need one to snorkel. For permit information, contact the Bermuda Department of Marine and Ports, 441-295-6575.

The **Wychwood** was an English freighter built in 1950 at the Sunderland shipyard in England. She was a little more than 300 feet long, 45 feet across the beam, and she displaced some 2,500 tons. On the evening of August 11th, 1955, while on the way from Nova Scotia to Trinidad, she ran aground on the reef 10 miles off shore from the Gibbs Hill Lighthouse.

She was pulled off the reef by the United States Navy and taken under tow stern first. Her steering gear had been damaged by the rocks. She'd sprung her plates and was taking on water, but her pumps seemed to be handling the situation quite well. On August 13th, with the approach of hurricane Diana, her crew put her at anchor off Five Fathom's Hole and left her to ride out the storm on her own. On August 10th, her pumps were no longer able to cope with rising water and she sank.

Later, she was deemed a hazard to navigation and was blown up. Today, the remains lie scattered across the sea bed in 50 to 60 feet of water.

The **Zovetto** was built and launched in Glasgow, Scotland, at the end of the First World War in 1919. She was a fairly large freighter, almost 400 feet from bow to stern, with a displacement of 5,100 tons. She was sold to the Italian shipping company, Parodi & Accame out of Genoa, and renamed the Zorvetto.

On February 13th, 1924, she was bound for Baltimore out of the Black Sea port of Poti with a cargo of manganese ore when she ran onto the reef while being piloted through the channel of St. David's. Her crew all made it safely off the ship and her cargo was salvaged.

Today, she lies in shallow waters less than a mile south of St. David's point off the eastern end of the island.

Dive Operators

There are a half-dozen professional dive operators in Bermuda; all of them can be relied upon to offer a variety of services in an efficient, safe and professional manner.

Many of the large hotels have their own watersports facilities and rental equipment for use by guests of other hotels. They will be pleased to arrange diving excursions with one or another of the dive operators. There is a decompression chamber at the King Edward Memorial Hospital on Point Finger Road in Paget.

All rates and packages quoted below were correct at the time of writing but are, as always, subject to change without notice.

BLUE WATER DIVERS LTD., at Robinson's Marina, Somerset Bridge, Sandy's Parish, Bermuda, 441-234- 1034, www.divebermuda.com, operates daily year-round (including holidays), from 7:30 am until 6 pm. Dive trips and excursions begin at 9:30 am and 1:30 pm. Blue Water Divers offers a range of courses from beginner to instructor to simple snorkeling – call for current rates.

Wet suits, when necessary, are provided at no extra charge. The location and the times of dives are subject to change according to the local weather conditions. Group rates are available for six persons or more, and night dives can also be arranged. Non-divers can accompany their partners for a fee of $12 per person.

DIVE BERMUDA, at 6 Dockyard Terrace, PO Box SB 246, Sandy's Parish, Bermuda, SB 8X, _441-234-1034, operates daily from March through December, and periodically in January and February, from 8 am until 6 pm, including holidays. Dive times are 10 am and 2 pm. Dive Bermuda also offers a full range of courses from beginner to instructor to simple snorkeling – call for current rates.

TRIANGLE DIVING at Grotto Bay, 441-293-7319; 11 Blue Hole Hill, Bailey's Bay, Bermuda CRO4 www.trianglediving.com. This outfit offers a full range of courses and excursions to shipwrecks and is located at the Grotto Bay resort just outside of St. Georges and less than 20 minutes from the airport. Call for current rates and offerings.

Swimming & Snorkeling

The shallow waters within the reef are renowned for their clarity. If you like to swim and snorkel, you can stop virtually anywhere on one of the coast roads, park your moped or bicycle, walk a short distance, and find yourself on a sandy beach with a vast expanse of deep blue ocean stretching into the distance.

For snorkeling, the south side of the island group is the easiest and most accessible. The beaches, bays and inlets offer numerous possibilities and the best spots are only as far away as the nearest beach. Swimming and snorkeling abound along the coast road to St. George's, the east end of the island from Achilles Bay to Buildings Bay, a 12-mile line of beaches on the South Shore from John Smith's Bay in the east to Church Bay in the west, and from Devil's Head Beach Park to the Mangrove Marina at the extreme northwest tip of the island.

To the west, around St. George's, there's Whale Bone Bay, Tobacco Bay, Achilles Beach Park, and the beaches just south of St. Catherine's Point. From West Whale Bay all along the south coast as far as John Smith's Bay to the east, you can just about take your pick and you won't be disappointed. The short stretch of water from and including Horseshoe Bay to Jobson's Cove offers some of the most spectacular snorkeling. Go when the water is quiet and watch out for sudden surges that can wash you onto the rocks.

Church Bay on the South Shore and Shell Bay on the North Shore are particularly well suited to snorkeling, and the beaches there are regarded as some of the best on the islands. Mangrove Bay, Long Bay and the beaches just north of Ely's Harbour also offer splendid snorkeling, as do those off Spanish Point. Snorkeling equipment is available for rent at most of the major hotels and dive shops around the island – see the Diving chapter as well as Equipment Rental. You will also find that most charter boats rent equipment.

Golf

Would you believe that Bermuda has more golf courses than it does fast food restaurants? That's what they claim. And, to tell the truth, it's something I had never really thought about but, you know, I think it might well be true. There are almost no fast food restaurants on Bermuda that I can think of, and that includes the City of Hamilton. If it is true, then that fact alone makes Bermuda a very extraordinary destination –

golf or not. What is true is that Bermuda, with nine golf courses, has the highest concentration of golfing opportunities per square mile in the world.

Bermuda's golf courses seem to have distinct personalities all their own. Many of them are in remote locations where an unpredictable wind blows constantly in off the Atlantic Ocean making even the seemingly simplest club selection nothing less than a lottery. Golf in Bermuda is always a pleasure. There's no rising before dawn to stand in line; rarely will you have long to wait on any tee. You'll play a game at your own pace; other players do not try to rush you from behind. You'll have all the time in the world to contemplate that 40-foot putt. And there are no distractions, save for the occasional song of an exotic bird. If you stay for a week, you can play a different course every day and still have one left over. Many hotels offer special golf packages, and all stand ready to help you plan the rest of your stay around your golfing needs.

Golf can be enjoyed year-round, but there's something about the warm breezes of the early summer months that make the greens the most challenging, and the fairways the fairest. From October through March, everything is at its very best; the courses are in peak condition, tee times are readily available, and hotel rates are low. January through March, there are "Golf Weeks" in Bermuda (see below). Each month during this period, a week is set aside for a variety of tournaments tailored to golf enthusiasts of all ages and of every skill level. Visit www.bermudagolf.org for more information.

Automated Reservation System: 441-234-4653.

Dress Code

Shirts must have collars and sleeveless shirts are prohibited. Shorts must be Bermuda length (to the knee) and jeans and cut-offs are absolutely not allowed.

Tee-Times

Reservations at the three government-run courses – Ocean View, Port Royal and St George's – can be made by calling the central reservation system at 441-234 4653. Tee times at the other courses can be made through hotels or by contacting the course directly.

Three of the courses are private clubs – Mid Ocean, Riddell's Bay and Tucker's Point – so you'll need either an introduction by a member or a stay at one of the many hotels that have corporate memberships and are able to introduce a limited number of their guests. Many of the cruise ships visiting Bermuda offer a round of golf as part of their shore excursion program.

Groups & Tournament Play

Most courses will accommodate groups if the Director of Golf or golf club management is notified well in advance. Special group green fees, however, are not normally offered. If your group is playing a tournament in Bermuda, you are eligible to receive local prizes, compliments of the Bermuda Department of Tourism, provided arrangements are made in advance. The maximum group qualification is 20 players.

Golf Equipment Golf clubs, both left- and right-handed are available at each course. Balls at most leading stores in Bermuda cost between $15 and $60 per dozen. They are priced slightly higher in the club pro shops.

Reseeding Greens

Reseeding is usually done between late September and early November, depending on weather conditions. Some courses go to temporary greens for a period of two to four weeks, others keep their greens in play. Check with your hotel or golf course during this period to determine what the local conditions might be.

Special Charges for Golfing Equipment on Airlines

Airlines differ regarding policies on golf bags. Some will include them as a part of your free baggage allowance, others charge a flat fee. Check with your airline before you make a reservation.

The Courses

Tiny, elevated greens are often guarded by sand traps placed with glee by architects such as Robert Trent Jones to punish even the slightest wayward shot. Greens and tee provide spectacular views of the ocean, rock shorelines, and pristine pink, sandy beaches. Irrigation on these often spectacular courses is limited, which means that the greens and fairways are always firmer and faster than those found elsewhere around the world. Finally, as you may well imagine, water plays a huge part in the layout of almost all of Bermuda's golf courses. Windswept cliff tops, steep ocean drop-offs, and breathtaking views are the highlights of play everywhere.

Belmont Hills Golf Club in Warwick, 441-236-6400, www.belmonthills.com. Belmont is a par 70, 18-hole course of 5,600 yards. The green fees (which include golf carts) are $95 Monday through Friday, $105 on weekends.

The pros are Darron Swan and Brian Morris. Elevated greens and double-tiered greens, blind second shots, tight fairways and small, narrow greens make it a challenging round. Golfers with handicaps of 10 or less should be able to shoot in 70s.... but don't bet on it!

Belmont Hills Golf Club
Courtesy of the Bermuda Dept. of Tourism

Tucker's Point Golf Club in Tucker's Town, 441-298-6959, www.tuckerspoint.com, is a par 70, 18-hole course of 6,440 yards. The green fee is $150, a cart for 18 holes $26 per person.

Tucker's Point Golf Club
Courtesy of the Bermuda Dept. of Tourism

The pro is Kevin Benevides. Castle Harbour offers a magnificent panorama of the surrounding countryside and the turquoise waters. It has more than 6,000 yards of undulating terrain, brought into play by architect Charles Banks. The resort-style championship course requires straight drives and well-placed second shots to heavily guarded greens, where a keen eye and a courageous spirit will help keep your score in check. Introduction by member required.

The Mid-Ocean Golf Club in Tucker's Town, 441-293-8837, www.themidoceanclubbermuda.com, is a par 71, 18-hole course of 6,547 yards. The green fee is $200 ($70 if you play with a member), a cart for 18 holes $70.

The Mid Ocean Golf Club – Courtesy Bermuda Dept. of Tourism

The pro is Keith Pearman. Experts rate Mid-Ocean among the top links in the world. And, as with any great course, good shots are rewarded and bad shots are penalized. Six of the par fours exceed 400 yards, and there's even a par 3 of 238 yards. It's a very tough course, so don't expect to score well the first time out. The club features some of the most spectacular views on the islands. You'll need an introduction by a member if you want to play Mid- Ocean. Drop by the pro shop and see if you can find a willing soul.

Ocean View Golf Club in Devonshire, 441-295-9092, is a par 35, nine-hole course of 2,956 yards. The green fee is $80 for 18 holes, cart included. The pro is Duane Pearman. Ocean View is owned and maintained by the Government of Bermuda. Measuring less than 3,000 yards, it seems somewhat tame at first. But players soon realize that the unpredictable terrain and rambling hills and dales make it very challenging. Score well here, and you should go home satisfied.

Port Royal Golf Course in Southampton, 441- 234-0974, fax 441-234- 3562, prgc@bermudagolf. bm, www.portroyalgolf. bm. Home of the Grand Slam of Golf played in October each year.

The Famous 16th at Port Royal Golf Club
Courtesy of the Bermuda Dept. of Tourism

Regular fee is $145 per round, plus a cart fee of $32. Sunset, usually after 3pm depending upon the season, starts at $78 per round, including cart and practice balls; club rentals – a bit stiff at $50.

All the expected amenities are at hand. There's a full-service pro shop where you can rent clubs and shoes. Port Royal is a Bermuda Government course operated by the Bermuda Ministry of Tourism. As municipal courses go, it's one of the finest I've ever seen. Designed by Robert Trent Jones and opened in 1970, it plays a tough par 71 of 6,561 yards off the back tees, and is a testament to its designer's genius.

Your round starts with a tough par 4, dog leg right of 432 yards and from there it proceeds, twisting and turning as it meanders along through woodland, meadow, seashore and cliff top with some of the most spectacular vistas on the island. The 4th – a shortish par 4 of 403 yards – handicapped 1, is the toughest hole on the course. It's a slight dog leg right, which in itself is not so much of a problem, especially if your natural tendency is to fade the ball. But that, unfortunately, is the problem.

Mr. Jones foresaw that and placed bunkers in the crook of the elbow of the dog leg at 235 yards and 263 yards, right where that nicely faded ball is sure to finish. Then, of course, there's the green itself: bunkers to the front left and right and to the right rear – again in just the right place to capture that nicely faded ball.

Number 11, handicapped 2, is also a score killer. It plays straight down the middle, but the fairway is narrow and there's a nasty patch of rough right in the landing area at about 200 yards out from the back tee, 160 yards from the white tee, and it stretches for 20 or 30 yards. From there, though, all you have to do is hit the small, elevated green; simple enough, except for the five bunkers that guard it right and left. The 15th is yet another spectacular ocean-side hole. At only 384 yards off the back tee (337 off the white tee), it would seem to be not too much of a challenge. Hmmm...

Not so, I'm afraid. With trees all the way along the fairway to the right, and nothing but ocean and spectacular drop-offs bounding the left side, you simply have to hit the fairway with your tee shot if you're to have any chance of making a par. And, talking of spectacular, there's none quite as heart-stopping as Port Royal's signature hole: the Par 3, 176-yard 16th. Yep, it's one of those delightfully intimidating stretches where there's nothing between you on the tee and the green but ocean and rocks. And then, even if you manage to negotiate the "gap," the green is heavily guarded on all sides by bunkers strategically placed by the erstwhile Mr. Jones.

Finally, one of the toughest finishing holes I've ever come across is the par 4, 405-yard 18th. From an elevated tee, it's uphill all the way. The temptation is to under-club. If you do, the hole could mean a disastrous finish to an otherwise respectable score, always supposed you made it through 16 with the same ball you started with. So, the game-plan is to take at least one more club than you otherwise would. Oh, and don't be long – the back of the green is heavily bunkered.

When the golf has been played, the clubs stowed away, and the shower taken, all that's left is to talk about the game we just played – what went wrong, what went right – over a pint or two of best draft beer. And, I can tell you this, there are a few club houses I've been to with more spectacular views than those from Port Royal Clubhouse (441-234-5037), but not many. The food is typical golf club fare: steaks and such for dinner (with chips, of course) and it's open for breakfast and lunch too.

Fairmont Princess Golf Club in Southampton, 441-238-0446, www.fairmont.com/southampton, is a par 3, 18-hole course of 2,740 yards for a total par of 54. The green fee is $90, a cart for 18 holes $35 for guests and $30 for others; hand-carts $6.

Fairmont Southampton Golf Club - Copyright Blair Howard

The pro is Bruce Simms. The Princess is a course with a difference. Located on the grounds of the Princess Hotel, it commands one of the highest and most scenic settings on the islands.

When the wind blows, the seemingly easy course becomes something of nightmare, and even on the balmiest of days it requires skillful ironwork, rather than sheer power. Playing here will reintroduce you to every club in your bag. The par 3 Princess presents a challenge for every golfer, with elevated tees and strategically placed water and bunkers.

Riddles Bay Golf & Country Club in Warwick, 441-238-1060, www.riddellsbay.com, is a par 69, 18-hole course of 5,588 yards. The green fee – please call. The pro is Darron Swan. Riddell's Bay is Bermuda's oldest golf club. For almost 80 years golfers from around the world have enjoyed this peninsula course where the fairways are tight, the greens small and narrow, the traps unforgiving, and the ocean itself is an opponent to be reckoned with. You'll need an introduction by a member or your hotel management to play at Riddell's Bay.

St. George's Golf Course, in St. George's Parish, 441-234-4653; www.tee.bm. Reopened in June 2011 as a budget play course. St. George's Golf Course, windswept and hauntingly beautiful, is located at one of the most remote spots on the island. The wind blows steadily in off the ocean almost all the time, making club choice more of a lottery than a science – on two of the par 3's it could be anything from a 9-iron to a driver – I am not kidding. It's also one of the shortest courses on the island, playing just 4,043 yards – a mere par-62, but a full 18 holes none-the-less.

The signature hole is the 326 yard, par 4 14th hole, a radical dog leg that hooks around Coot Pond (not really a pond at all, but a scenic little harbor dotted with private boats and providing a view over the ocean beyond that the word stunning only barely describes). When the prevailing wind is from the north, you may be tempted to launch your ball out over the waters of the Coot and go directly for the green, thus foregoing the fairway and its 90-degree dog leg. If you do, and if you make it, you'll effectively cut the hole down to a par 3. If you don't make it, well... And, talking of the greens, they are all small, very small. This course defines the term "target golf." Fort St. George dominates number 4, a somewhat deceivingly short par 4 just 305 yards off the back tee that dog-legs to the right. The ominous Fort St. Catherine, which was built to protect Bermuda from the Spaniards in the 17th century, guards the 16th.

By now you'll have figured it out that I love this little, windswept course at the edge of the world, and you would be right, I do. If you're going to play golf in Bermuda, you must put St. George's at the top of your play list. Oh, and don't forget to take your camera. St. George's is a government-run course operated by the Ministry of Tourism and, as its name implies, situated near the historic town of St George which in itself is well worth a visit: don't forget to check out Sir George Sommers' pioneering ship The Deliverance, and the town square where you'll find all sorts of neat things to see and do. 18 holes cost $60 with reduced rates after 3 p.m. in summer and 1 p.m. in the winter. Golf carts are mandatory on weekends and public holidays, otherwise pull carts can be rented for $8.

The Clubhouse has a fully stocked Pro Shop (441-234-4653) and Locker Room. The Restaurant and Lounge offers ocean views over the North Atlantic Shore and the 18th green. Proper golf attire is required at all time, both on the course and in the clubhouse, and soft spiked golf shoes are mandatory. As with the other government-run courses, Ocean View and Port Royal, reservations can be made through an automated reservation system by calling 441-234-4653.

Spas

Please note: All prices quoted were current at the time of writing and are subject to change, and change they do, almost weekly. That being so, the prices quoted herein are given only to give you an idea of what to expect.

Willow Stream Spa at the Fairmont Southampton, Southampton, 800-441-1414 or 441-239-6924, www.willowstream.com. Willow Stream Spa is an elegant and peaceful haven in one of Bermuda's grand luxury resorts.

In a surrounding of breathtaking beauty, the serene setting of this adult sanctuary is the perfect venue for reclaiming your power and rekindling your spirit. Whether you are looking to pamper your face with an ultimate facial (90 min., $259), detoxify your body in a thermal mineral bath (30 min., $79) or indulge in a full body experience that will leave you radiating from head to toe, this full-service spa is sure to indulge even the highest expectations. Willow Stream Spa also offers a number of services geared specifically towards the avid golf enthusiast (an 18-hole championship golf course is on site).

The hydrating golf facial (90 min., $229) was designed to brighten the skin and help repair skin damaged by the elements. The signature Golf Treatment Massage (60 min., $199), endorsed by world-class professional golf instructor David Leadbetter, is said to aid in improving golf performance and swing rotation for distance and accuracy.

Relaxing on the sundeck, a refreshing dip in the spa pool or a stroll in the traditional Bermuda gardens perfumed with the natural aromatherapy of the island will continue to nourish your soul long after you have returned home. Full spa access is complimentary on the day of a spa treatment of $99 or more. Amenities include: 15 spa treatment rooms, fitness facility, inhalation and sauna, steam room, Spa Pool with Jacuzzis, and a sundeck; product lines available: Kerstin Florian, Willow Stream Energy and Balance and B. Kamins.

The Spa at Elbow Beach, Paget Parish, 800-223-7434, www.mandarinoriental.com/Bermuda. The Spa at Elbow Beach is an ultimate indulgence, even for the jet setters of the world. While you may enjoy treatments that radiate with true Bermudian flair, such as the Soothing Aloe and Bermuda Honey Envelopment, the Taste of Traditions facial and body treatments will guide you to ancient traditions and techniques inspired by different corners of the globe, including India, Arabia, the Orient and the Mediterranean.

Signature services on the menu of holistic therapies include the Oriental Harmony Massage, where four hands work in perfect unison to make each part of your body come alive in a delightful sizzle. If you are in need of rejuvenating your body's equilibrium, then you might want to give the Chakra balancing with hot stones a try.

Each one of the six private spa suites is decorated in soothing colors with Asian accents and features a handcrafted Granite soaking tub. Breathtaking views of the Atlantic Ocean may be enjoyed from the comfort of a private balcony.

This spa is a 'must experience' for anyone desiring tranquil seclusion in order to reenergize the spirit and soul. 6 Private Spa Suites including two couples suites, state-of the- art fitness center, pool, private beach, tennis courts, and special Spa cuisine. Product Lines: ESPA, MO Signature.

The Ocean Spa at Cambridge Beaches, Sandy's Parish, 800-468-7300, www.cambridgebeaches.com. Enjoy all the amenities and facilities of a beautiful resort in combination with a world-class spa. If you've never been to a spa before, this is a great place for you to have your first experience.

The spa is world-class; the treatments include a wide range of Spas offerings from classic massages to body treatments and facials utilizing the famous Sothys of Paris line of products, to marine-based body wraps and holistic therapies. Yoga classes are offered year-round and, in between experiences, you can relax and unwind in the quiet confines of the Ocean Spa's Meditation gardens.

Inverurie Day Spa at the Fairmont Hamilton Princess, Hamilton, 441-239-6924, www.fairmont.co m/hamilton. I love the official intro to this spa: "Indulge and treat your senses and your skin to an exotic skin care line that brings together superior quality Hungarian ingredients with old world knowledge of herbs, fruits and essences. All ingredients are organically grown and hand-picked in Hungary." Now if that doesn't excite the inveterate spa aficionado, I don't know what will.

The Inverurie Spa really is an opportunity for you to "experience the unusual." The spa's signature treatment is the "couples massage," and you can take it poolside in your own personal tent while sharing a glass of champagne overlooking Hamilton Harbor. Then, when the treatments are complete, you can conclude this truly extravagant delight with a customized dining experience on the balcony of your room. Thai Massage. You have a choice of treatments – 55 or 85 minutes. This form of massage incorporates ancient healing techniques from traditional masters based on the theory that invisible lines of force run throughout the body. Practitioners use hands, feet, elbows, knees and legs to stretch, balance and exercise one's being. Pressure is applied to acupressure points, encouraging the release of toxins from the body. The effects are immediate and lasting both spiritually and physically. No oils and/or creams are used in this treatment.

Horseback Riding

Horseback riding is possible throughout the year at the two commercial stables listed below. Both cater to experienced and novice riders, and all rides are accompanied by qualified instructors. Horses cannot be hired and ridden without supervision, as Bermuda has very strict laws regarding horseback riding in public areas, especially on the public beaches. Advance reservations are required at both stables.

Horseback Riding Stables

The Lee Bow Riding Centre, Tribe Road #1, Devonshire, Bermuda DV O6, 441-236-4181, caters to juniors of all experience levels (to the age of 18). They offer instruction by qualified equestrian instructors throughout the day. The Centre has an outdoor arena.

Lessons are available by reservation; call for hourly rates. Small groups may book ahead for trail rides.

The Spicelands Riding Centre, Middle Road, Warwick, 441-238-8212, www.spicelandsriding.com, is set in a rural area close to the South Shore. A bridle path leads from the Riding Center to the beach, and a full staff of qualified personnel caters to the needs of riders. They take children and adults at all levels of expertise. A number of daily trail rides are available by reservation:

Breakfast Rides at 6:45 each morning head along the South Shore beaches and bridle paths. The rides last for about 1½ hours, and the rate includes a continental breakfast after the ride.

Trail Rides along the South Shore last for about an hour and begin at 10 am, 11:30am and 3 pm.

Evening Rides are conducted Monday through Friday from May through September. Protective headgear is provided; hard-soled shoes or sneakers are recommended. The rates are always subject to change, so please call ahead to verify current charges. Visa, MasterCard or American Express cards are required when making a reservation, and 24-hour's notice is required for cancellation.

Bermuda Riding for the Disabled, Windreach Recreation Village, 5 Wind Reach Lane, 441-238-7433. This facility has only been open for a couple of years, but it's fast gaining in popularity. Here, handicapped adults and kids can enjoy an experience they may never have the opportunity for anywhere else. All are welcome. Lessons and riding are provided free of charge – it's a charitable organization – but donations are welcome and appreciated. As it's one of the more popular attractions on the islands, you should call well ahead of time to book your spot. The facility is completely wheelchair-accessible. Open Monday through Friday from 9:30 am to 3 pm, and on Saturday from 9:30 until noon.

For more information about the various equestrian opportunities on the islands, you can contact the Bermuda Equestrian Federation, 441-295-6042. They will give you all the information you need on scheduled events – show jumping and the like – throughout the year.

Shopping

There are four main shopping areas in Bermuda: the City of Hamilton, St. George's, Somerset Village and the Royal Naval Dockyard. Most of them have been covered in the section on sightseeing. Despite the small size of the island, you won't be disappointed by the high number of sophisticated, multi-story department stores, specialty shops, gift stores, jewelry outlets and perfumeries on the main streets and waterfronts of all four areas, not to mention the hidden shops tucked away all around the islands.

Front Street - Courtesy of the Bermuda Dept. of Tourism

Service in retail stores is, for the most part, helpful and courteous. Sometimes, however, the pressures of the tourist industry will overcome even the most patient of service personnel, who tire toward the end of the day and whose tempers can become a little ragged. This doesn't happen often, but if it does, just smile and pass right along. There's always another store just down the road. The best bargains in Bermuda are goods imported from Europe. Such items as Italian, German, English and French knitwear can often be purchased at prices far below those in the United States. Watches (Rolex, Omega, Patek Philippe), jewelry, French perfumes,

Icelandic woolen goods, and fine china can be 50cheaper than at home.

The City of Hamilton

Shops not to be missed include Cooper's Shop in Hamilton. On Front Street, try Constables of Bermuda for Icelandic woolens, The Irish Linen Shop, Astwood Dickinson (fine jewelry), and Bluck's for fine china and paintings. Others are the Bridge House Straw Market in St. George's for hats and bags and the Washington Mall on Queen Street between Reid and Church Street in Hamilton.

The **Washington Mall** is the only shopping mall in the city. It features a variety of boutiques, restaurants and film and digital processing. So let's take a closer look at some of the possibilities. We'll start in Hamilton. Perhaps the most obvious place to go shopping in the city is the Washington Mall. Yes, it's a mall in every sense of the American definition: long avenues of shops, stores, cafés and the like that connect one city thoroughfare to another.

There are three sections: the Mall itself, then West Washington Mall and Washington Mall II. The Mall and its Western section are both entered from Reid Street. Be sure to stop in at Delicious: there you'll find such delicacies as cream slices (made with real cream) and sausage rolls. If you're from England, you'll know exactly what sausage rolls are. If not, you should try one. They're something of an acquired taste and not everyone likes them. However, a sausage roll and a cup of hot tea always tops my list of priorities – when I can find one, that is.

Inside the Mall, you'll find a wealth of shopping opportunities, including the Body Shop, another English legend, the Harbourmaster for fine leather goods, and a number of little shops where you can get those hard-to-find gifts for the folks back home. Butterfield Place, off

Front Street in Hamilton, is a unique little shopping center with all sorts or upscale goodies, including leather goods at Voila, Scottish woolens at the Highlander, fine arts at the Michael Swann Gallery; there's even a Louis Vuitton outlet. Next to Butterfield Place, still on Front Street, is The Emporium, another unique grouping of small shops and stores. If you're a cigar aficionado, stop in at the Tienda de Tabaco; you might even want to take time out to enjoy a smoke with the regulars.

It's difficult to describe what kind if niche A.S. Cooper, 59 Front Street in Hamilton, fills. I suppose it's best described as an upscale gift shop, though that hardly does it justice. Anyway, here you'll see all sorts of fine gifts to take home. These might include a bone china teapot, a unique piece of jewelry, or a bottle of exotic perfume. There are branches on Reid Street in Hamilton, on Somer's Wharf in St. George, in the Southampton Princess, the Elbow Beach Hotel, and at the Royal Naval Dockyard. 441- 295-3961.

Bluck's is where to go when you're looking for fine china. The main store is on Front Street in Hamilton, and there are branches in St. George and at the Southampton Princess Hotel. Many of the designs have been commissioned from the great potteries in Europe especially for Bermuda. These include Spode, Worcester, Staffordshire and Herend. 441-295-5367.

The Irish Linen Shop, at Hey's Corner, 31 Front Street, in Hamilton, is another opportunity you won't want to miss. I can assure you, my wife never does. Wherever we go, she makes this outlet one of her first ports of call; yes, you can find them in Freeport and Nassau in the Bahamas, as well as on some of the islands in the Caribbean. Our dining table is always covered by a fine linen table cloth, along with napkins and placemats. The beds have Irish linen pillow cases, and the sideboard usually sports a linen mat of one sort or another. The great thing about these shops is the prices: always, you'll pay at least 40less for your linens than you would at home. Better yet, if you happen to visit them when they're running a sale, you can walk away, loaded up, feeling as if you've just robbed the store. 441-295-4089, fax 441- 295-4089.

Be sure to stop by the Gem Cellar and take a look at their handmade jewelry. Again, if you're looking for that one-of-a-kind gift, this old-world little jeweler's shop is where you'll probably find it. Take Old Cellar Lane from Front Street in Hamilton. 441-292-3042.

The Clocktower Mall

The Clock Tower Mall in Sandy's Parish, 441- 234-3342. To me, the best thing about this place is its overpowering historical atmosphere. It's not been too long since this whole area was bustling with thousands of British seamen, and it still shows. The great Clocktower building is as intimidating today as it must have been a hundred years ago. I've spent many an hour wandering the lower and upper galleries of this great stone edifice; it borders on the hypnotic. But I can't say that I've been that impressed, with a couple of notable exceptions, by the shops therein and what they have to offer. Everything seems a little contrived, geared toward separating the visitor from his/her money.

There are some 30 shops and stores in this rather strange mall that some have compared favorably with the Burlington Arcade in London. I don't agree. Prices in the mall are generally on the high side. Even so, if you take into account that it's all tax-free, you're probably going to walk away with a bargain or two.

AS to the shops themselves, it seems they have a lot of turnover; shops and stores come and go, and you're never quite sure what you'll find each time you visit.

The Clock Tower Mall - Courtesy of the Bermuda Dept. of
Tourism

There are, of course, many more shopping
opportunities on the islands, and half the fun is in
digging them out. Take time to wander the shops in St.
George; you won't be disappointed. Get out and about
among the side streets in Hamilton, and don't be afraid
to get off the beaten path in the parishes. There's a
pleasant surprise just around almost every corner

Where to Eat

Dining in Bermuda can be as formal or as fancy free as you like and you can choose a different dining style every day of the week. One day you can feast on fresh seafood served at the water's edge, another you can settle back in a plush, cosmopolitan setting and enjoy a meal of French or Italian cuisine. You might like to travel back in time and dine at a century-old Bermudian restaurant, embark on a romantic evening at sea on a starlit dinner cruise, or relax in an English-style pub where the menu is listed on a chalkboard.

And then, of course, there's the old British tradition of afternoon tea. Every day, at precisely four o'clock in the afternoon, Bermudians stop for tea. They drink a variety of brews and nibble on tiny sandwiches, breads, jams, pastries and, of course, scones and clotted cream. It's a tradition most visitors enjoy, even if it does mean leaving the sun and sand for an hour or two.

The Old and The New

The restaurants and cafés in Bermuda are as varied as they are many. Unfortunately, the restaurants in Bermuda, like the shops and stores, seem to come and go with the wind, but one or two of the long established, and even famous, establishments are still in business and just as good as ever. Thus it's virtually impossible to keep up with what's going on in Bermuda's restaurant industry. The being so, much to the dismay of some, I have kept my choices of restaurants in Bermuda to just the few tried and true Institutions; those that have been around for many a year and, no doubt, will be around for many more.

So, here and there, I've added some thoughts as to value and recommendation. If I've recommended a restaurant or café, you can be sure it was worth recommending at the time of writing. If it's not up to par when you visit, or if it's gone out of business, I would like to know about it. Please feel free to write to me via e-mail at blair@blairhoward.com. And, as always, the prices quoted were current at the time of writing, but they are always subject to change, and they do, almost weekly, but the prices quoted herein will give you an idea of what to expect.

Dress in restaurants is mostly casual/smart – trousers and a casual shirt for men; slacks and blouse or a dress for ladies; no shorts, tee-shirts or swimwear. All restaurants, unless otherwise stated, accept most major credit cards.

Restaurant Price Scale:

$$$+ Over $50 per person

$$ $20-$50 per person

$ Under $25 per person

$$$ **Ascot's**, 24 Rosemont Avenue, Pembroke, 441-295- 9644. Newly renovated and extended, a verandah restaurant open every day for dinner: seafood, chicken, steaks, homemade cheesecake, desserts and sauces.

$$ The **Carriage House**, Somer's Wharf, St. George's, 441-297-1270. A cozy, vaulted brick dining room in historic St. George's. Open seven days a week for dinner: seafood, beef, dessert trolley. $ Chopsticks, Reid Street, Hamilton, 441-292-0791. A restaurant serving Chinese and Thai dishes. Open for dinner seven days a week.

$$$ **Fourways Inn Restaurant**, Middle Road, Paget Parish, 441-236-6517. An elegant restaurant serving classic and contemporary French cuisine. Live entertainment. Jacket and tie required. Menu changes daily.

$$-$$$ **The Freeport** Seafood Restaurant, Royal Naval Dockyard, Sandy's Parish, 441-234-1692. This great little seafood restaurant has been one of my favorites ever since I began writing about Bermuda, and

that's some 16 years ago now. If you visit the Royal Naval Dockyard, you'd be remiss if you didn't do dinner at the Freeport.

They serve only the best of locally caught seafood. No fish & chips here, and no flare for the dramatic, just good, plain-old sea food cooked just the way you like it and served quickly, hot and without fuss. Try their signature fish platter or maybe you'd like to try the broiled Bermuda rockfish – that one I can personally recommend.

For lunch, if you can't stay for dinner, you'll find they serve all the regular goodies, including burgers, salads, pizzas, and steak on the grill. Best of all, at least on the lunch menu, is the fish sandwich.

The dinner menu includes some old favorites, such as steaks, chicken and pork. But it's the seafood menu that the Freeport is famous for. The fish selection changes with the seasons and might include anything from tuna to wahoo. They even serve lobster, but it runs a bit pricy for me, and I never was a big fan of the spiny critter anyway.

An added bonus is that the restaurant has now joined the cyber world and is, in fact, an internet café with computers customers can use. Believe it or not, though, they don't have a website. Open for lunch and dinner seven days a week.

$-$$ **Frog & Onion**, The Cooperage, Royal Naval Dockyard, 441-234-2900, www.frogandonion.bm .This has long been one of my favorites. A British-style pub set inside what once was the barrel-making factory for the British Royal Navy, it really does have a little of the old-English atmosphere that's hard to find now, even in the country pubs of the UK. The specialty is English beer, expensive at $4.75 a pint, but the real thing: Newcastle Brown, Watney's, Flower's, all on draft, along with that good old Irish mainstay, Guinness. I love

Guinness and was surprised to find that this was one of the few establishments on Bermuda that bothers to stock it.

I read a book once whose hero claimed he had only three reasons for living: the fear of death, Goldie Hawn (no, it's not Kurt Russell), and Guinness. I know what he means. The food at the Frog & Onion is your basic pub fare: pies, fish and chips and a variety of sandwiches.

For dessert, you might like to try their English trifle. Open daily for lunch and dinner until midnight. Reservations not required. Take number 7 or 8 bus from Hamilton, or the ferry from all points around the Great Sound.

$$$ **The Harbourfront** – BUEI, Pembroke Hall, 40 Crow Lane, Pembroke, 441-295-4207. The Harbourfront Restaurant has recently moved to its new location right on the harbor at the Bermuda Underwater Exploration Institute (BUEI). The new dining room is certainly an improvement over the old one, but it's the stunning view over the harbor that makes it so special.

Even the move away from Hamilton has not diminished the restaurant's popularity, which means it can get very busy at times, especially on weekends. The menu remains much the same, and the owners still boast of offering the "freshest fish and seafood." A 14oz, dry aged sirloin strip steak with potatoes and assorted veggies will cost 192 Where to Eat $36.95; 18 ounces of New Zealand Rack of lamb with all the trimmings is $35.50; the Porterhouse Steak, a whopping 42 ounces, on the bone, with potatoes and veggies is a mere $89.00.

If you like Sushi, this is the place to get it. Caviar? They do that too. Gentlemen are expected to wear a jacket for dinner. Reservations are a must. Open for lunch from 11:45 am to 4 pm, and for dinner from 6 pm to 10pm; closed Sundays.

$$ **The Hog Penny**, Burnaby Hill, Hamilton, 441-292-2434, www.hogpennypub.com. This is my personal favorite place to eat in Bermuda. If you happen to claim English nationality, you'll know exactly what I mean when I say this is what the pubs used to be like back in the days in England. Unfortunately these days, you'll need to travel the length and breadth of England to find anything that even comes close to the once prevalent English pub.

And, if you are English, and can remember the old-style pubs, you'll also understand the feeling of déja vu I had when I walked into the Hog Penny a few weeks ago. It was like stepping back it time, in another place, on a different continent, so authentic was the atmosphere.

The name of the pub is taken from the old Bermudan Hog Money, which was "the earliest British Colonial currency, and, as written by Governor Nathaniel Butler in his 1620 account The Historye of the Bermudaes or Summer Islands, was given its name because of it "having a hog stamped upon it on one side (in memory it should seem of the great number of wild swine found upon the Islands at their first discovery in 1609 by the shipwrecked crew of the Sea Venture), and was, in a scoff, termed by the people hogge money."

The coinage included the Shilling, Sixpence, Thrupence, and Two pence, and were all of similar design bearing on the obverse side the inscription "Sommer Ilands", a wild boar on a bed of corn cobs, and the coin's denomination. On the reverse was a three masted ship under full sail." Today, hog money is found only in museums, and rarely even then.

The pub that carries its name, however, is quite a different story. Established in 1957, the Hog Penny Restaurant and Pub was cobbled together from old Watney's pubs in England that were being withdrawn, and many of the mirrors and benches you see in front of (and underneath!) you date back to the early 1900's. Interestingly enough, the Hog Penny is the actual original inspiration for the "Cheers" Pub in Boston.

The Food is a mixture of typically Bermuda and English "pub grub" and includes, to name just a few of my favorites: Dark & Stormy Rock Fish: Pan fried rockfish with Gosling's Black Seal rum and ginger beer sauce, served with basmati rice Where to Eat 193 and sautéed vegetables – $26; Seafood Mixed Grill: three types of market seafood with a lemon-caper-parsley butter, basmati rice and daily vegetables - $23; Roast Rack of Lamb: rubbed in an island spice mix of allspice, nutmeg, cloves and cinnamon, served with a sweet potato mash, sautéed vegetables and finished with a tamarind shallot demi glace - $29; English-style Fish & Chips: fillets of grouper coated with beer batter and then fried crispy brown, served with French fries, fresh vegetables and tartar sauce $21; Shepard's Pie: ground sirloin is used in this most traditional of English dishes, seasoned to perfection and topped with gratinated fresh mashed potato - $18; No authentic English pub would be complete without the inevitable Steak and Kidney Pie: beef and kidney cooked in a rich red wine sauce in a short pastry crust and served with French fries and mixed vegetables.

Open 11:30 am until 3 pm for lunch, and from 5:30 pm to 10 pm for dinner. Reservations for dinner are a good idea – it's a busy pub.

$$-$$$ **The Lobster Pot**, 6 Bermudiana Road, Hamilton, 441-292- 6898. For more than 30 years, since it first opened in 1973, the Lobster Pot has been one of Bermuda's most popular places to dine. It's just a short bus ride from downtown Hamilton. I recommend you pay it a visit. Lobster is, of course, the specialty, and they serve both the Maine and Caribbean (spiny) varieties.

They also serve a wide variety of fresh fish and shellfish, including wahoo, tuna, rockfish, and hogfish, along with shrimp, mussels and chowder (the best you'll ever eat). The lobster dishes are expensive, but lobster's expensive everywhere nowadays, except for Maine and, even there it's not so cheap anymore. Anyway, for an inexpensive treat, try a fish sandwich, or some coconut shrimp, or some Creole shrimp.

Take a number 1, 2, 10 or 11 bus and ask the driver to drop you off at the Lobster Pot. If you intend to make it a dinner outing, it would be a good idea to make a reservation. Open for lunch Monday through Friday from 11:30 am, and for dinner daily from 5:30 pm until 11 pm.

$$$ **The Newport Room**, Southampton Fairmont Hotel, Southampton, 441-238-8000. The Newport Room has long been regarded as Bermuda's premier dining experience – it's the only AAA 5-diamond-rated restaurant outside of the United States. The menu features a combination of contemporary French cuisine with the finest of wines, all presented with style and elegance. The décor is nautical – an elegant, luxury yacht-styled environment.

The Newport Room is reminiscent of good times in Bermuda now long gone, the atmosphere is one of nostalgia, recalling scenes from the famous Newport Bermuda sailing races that began in 1938 from Newport, Rhode Island and are still held today. Men are required to wear jackets; a tie is suggested, but not mandatory, and reservations are a must. The Newport Room is somewhat understated, and it's certainly not for everyone. If you're looking for that one-off, romantic dinner, however.... Open for dinner daily from 6:30 pm to 10:00 pm.

$$-$$$ **Palms**, at Surf Side Beach Club, South Shore Road, Warwick, 441-236-7100, www.surfside.bm. An

intimate little hotel restaurant, loaded with atmosphere and good cheer. It overlooks a kidney-shaped swimming pool and the ocean beyond. The food is excellent, if a little expensive. Set Where to Eat 196 Where to Eat menus that change daily feature a variety of American and international cuisine and there's a fairly comprehensive wine list, for fine dining on a small scale. The meals I had there were all presented with style and panache. If they happen to have rack of lamb on the menu, or lamb chops, you can order either one with confidence; mine was the best I'd had in a long time. If you have time for a drink before dinner, you'll enjoy the cozy little bar adjacent to the restaurant. It, too, overlooks the pool and ocean; very relaxing. The restaurant seats 16 to 20 people, so reservations are a must. I highly recommend it. Dress for dinner is casual smart. Open for dinner daily from 5:30 until 9:30 pm.

$-$$ **Swizzle Inn**, 3 Blue Hole Hill, Bailey's Bay, 441-293- 1854, www.swizzleinn.com. Named for the rum swizzle drink, this is one of the oldest pubs in Bermuda and very much a down-to-earth restaurant where the food is mainly inexpensive (especially the burgers and sandwiches) and the atmosphere pleasant and relaxing. You can dine inside or out. Try the fish sandwich – it's one of the best I've ever eaten. And you should also try the bread pudding, which is out of this world. Burgers are, of course, popular with the lunchtime crowd and, though I've never tried them, they are claimed to be quite special. Dinner features more of the same, but bigger, with more of an emphasis on seafood. There's fish, shrimp and shellfish, plus there's curry as well. The Swizzle Inn is just a short bus ride from Hamilton via a number 1, 3, 10 or 11 bus. Reservations not required. Open daily from 11 am until midnight (1 am during the busy season).

$$$ **The Waterlot Inn**, Southampton Fairmont Hotel, Southampton, 441-238-8000, claims to be Bermuda's most historic restaurant. For more than 330 years, so they say, they have been serving guests steaks and seafood in one of the most breathtaking dockside settings you're ever likely to find. This traditional steakhouse has earned both the AAA Four Diamond and Wine Spectator Awards. They also offer an award-winning wine list and, if you're a cigar aficionado, they have a selection of cigars you won't want to miss. The restaurant is open daily for dinner from 6 pm until 10 pm. Reservations are suggested; men should wear jackets.

Where to Stay
Bermuda's Hotels and Resorts

Probably the most important question you'll have when planning your visit is, where to stay in Bermuda. Accommodations in Bermuda can be fairly expensive. Rates, on the whole, though, are on a par with those of the hotels in London, Paris and New York. So... where to stay in Bermuda? We hope this section will help you figure it out. Below, you'll find listings of most of Bermuda's resorts, hotels, guest houses and self-catering/housekeeping apartments.

First, let's talk about meal plans: In-house meals, when not a part of a plan, can be costly with breakfast running anywhere from $20 to $35, and dinner rarely less than $50. And talking of breakfast: if you've never had a "full English breakfast" it's an experience you won't want to miss.

All this might at first seem a little off-putting, but don't let it. Bermuda is one of those rare spots on the globe where you can enjoy life as it should be enjoyed. When the sun shines and the fresh breezes blow in through the window of your guest room - small hotel, guest house or grand resort - you'll be glad you decided to spend a little time on one of the most beautiful islands in the western hemisphere. I promise.

If you want to save money, try to visit in the off-season between November 1st and March 31st; you'll save around 40on your hotel room rate. A vacation during these months can offer some definite advantages. While many of the tourist-related services – the helicopter rides, charter boats, dive operators, etc. – close during winter and the water can be a little on the cool side, the weather is ideal for golf, tennis, sightseeing and shopping. Oh, and be sure to check out your options with Self-Catering Cottages and Apartments, it's a really great way to stay in Bermuda.

Most of the islands' accommodations are on the South Side (along with the best beaches, in Paget, Warwick and Southampton Parishes), and still more are around the harbor and on the inner shores of Great Sound, served by a regularly scheduled bus and ferry service into Hamilton. It matters little where your hotel is located. The island is small and nowhere is very far from anywhere. All areas are well served by public transportation.

Resorts, Hotels, Guest Houses and Cottage Price Scale:
$$$$ More than $250 per night
$$$ $150-$250 per night
$$ $100-$150 per night
$ Less than $100 per night

Some of the quoted hotel rates might be subject to an energy surcharge. All rates are subject to a 7.25hotel occupancy tax and do not include gratuities.

Meal Plans at Hotels

Most hotels offer a choice between MAP, BP or EP rates. Guest houses usually offer a choice of BP, CP or EP.

CP (Continental Plan): provides a continental breakfast

EP (European plan): denotes no set meal plan, although restaurant facilities are either on the property or nearby

BP (Bermudian Plan): offers room and full breakfast

AP (Modified American Plan): includes breakfast and dinner

FAP (Full American Plan): includes all meals.

Resort Hotels:

Cambridge Beaches Resort Bermuda

Cambridge Beaches is a unique, world-class cottage colony resort situated on its own private 25 acre peninsula in Bermuda. With 94 luxury, cottage style rooms and suites, five private beaches, the world-acclaimed European Wellness Center, extensive marine rentals, tennis courts, putting green, croquet lawns and internationally recognized gourmet cuisine, it's a world all its own set on a semi-tropical island. What could be better than that? Devoted to the philosophy of guests must have the ability to be as active as they want, when they want to be; or to do nothing at all and do it well; Cambridge Beaches is private and exclusive, perfect for romantics of any age.

The hotel management suggests that you: "Surrender to sunsets. Dream in the daylight. Discover serenity. Imagine a place where your only wake-up call is the sound of palm trees whispering in the breeze; where the only invitation is the soft morning music of the surf; where you have all the time in the world to spend with your love.... Explore a coral reef with colorful fish.

Reflect on passing clouds from pristine pink sands. Savor mouth-watering delights prepared for your pleasure. Dare to indulge every desire. Feel the cool cerulean water receive you, surround you, transform you." Okay, it's a little over the top, but barely. Cambridge Beaches is one of the most luxurious, secluded spots on the map where there's nothing more to do than relax, far away from the maddening rush of big city, or even small city, day-to-day strife and pain.

I have spent a few nights at Cambridge Beaches and I can tell you, even though it's a little out of the way at the west end of the island, if you're looking for idyllic times and pampered luxury, this is the place for you.

Practical Information:

$$$$ MAP BP

Cambridge Beaches Resort

30 Kings Point Road

Sandys MA02, Bermuda

441 234-0331

Elbow Beach Hotel, Bermuda

Elbow Beach is one of Mandarin Oriental's acclaimed luxury hotels. The resort sits on 50 acres of beautifully-landscaped gardens, a mere five minutes from the charming town of Hamilton, and overlooks a pristine beach of pink sand and the ocean. The newly refurbished resort now features 98 luxurious guestrooms and suites found in cottages spread amongst the grounds.

The newly refurbished guestrooms and suites have been enhanced with the addition of advanced in-room entertainment systems with 200 channels of complimentary hi-definition television and music programming, luxurious soft furnishings, including 300 thread count sheets and Mandarin Oriental bedding, iPod docking stations, personal espresso machines and upgraded bathroom facilities.

There are four restaurants on site offering a full range of cuisine, from casual to elegant. Particularly noteworthy are Lido, an award-winning restaurant featuring innovative Mediterranean cuisine and Mickey's Beach Bistro and Bar which sits directly on Elbow Beach with panoramic vistas of the turquoise ocean.

The Spa at Elbow Beach is also definitely worth a visit. There are four single and two couple private treatment suites, each featuring stunning ocean views, a hand-crafted, granite soaking tub, bamboo flooring and river pebble-lined steam shower.

Amenities include a recreation lounge, cycle livery, five championship tennis courts (three lighted for night play), putting green, dive shop, fitness room and temperature controlled swimming pool. Golf can be arranged at nearby courses. Water sports, boating and game fishing can be arranged by the hotel concierge.

Contact:

Elbow Beach Hotel: 60 South Shore Road, Paget Parish, Bermuda (441) 236 3535 - www.mandarinoriental.com/bermuda.

The Fairmont Hamilton Princess Resort

One of two grand resorts in Bermuda, the Fairmont Hamilton Resort is one of my all-time favorite places to stay. It's handy to Bermuda's first city, Hamilton, its harbor, the ferry and the buses, and that's not to mention the shopping. The Fairmont Hamilton is a luxury resort hotel in the true meaning of the words. Fondly referred to by Bermudians as "The Pink Palace," the hotel is a true, old-world gem with all the modern amenities you could ever want. Situated right on the picturesque natural harbor of Hamilton, it's the perfect

Built in a time when Bermuda was still one of Britain's colonies, the Fairmont Hamilton is all about the old world splendor that is Bermuda, even today. The Hamilton Princess was inspired by Princess Louise, the daughter of Queen Victoria. It's a symbol of all that Bermudians hold dear – genuine hospitality and timeless quality. There are 410 elegant and beautiful guest rooms and suites of varying sizes and decor, many with private balconies, overlooking the turquoise waters of the harbor dotted with colorful sailboats and sleek yachts.

The resort also offers a new 'Fairmont Gold' floor, which essentially is a hotel within a hotel that features private check-in and concierge, as well as special amenities, such as a private salon with honor bar, cocktail hour canapés, and complimentary breakfast.

The resort features a number of different restaurants that will satisfy even the most sophisticated palate. The meals prepared at Harley's are cooked to perfection and it's no surprise that this restaurant won the Best of Bermuda Gold Award in hotel dining. For travelers looking for a particularly romantic interlude, a candlelight dinner prepared by your very own butler on your private balcony would surely turn into a memory to cherish for a very long time. Afternoon tea, the true British kind and the best in Bermuda, I might add, at the

Heritage Court is an event that should not be missed by anyone visiting the island. From the British silver tea sets and Belgian fine china to Italian fine woven linens, everything about the afternoon tea spells elegance and luxury.

Heritage Court offers a large selection of fine rums and cigars available for smoking on the terrace. The facilities at this resort include a fitness center and an outdoor freshwater as well as an outdoor saltwater pool.

There is complimentary ferry service to its sister hotel, the Southampton Princess, which offers a private beach club, a golf course, 11 all-weather tennis courts (including seven lighted courts), fishing and water sports at the deep-water dock, and a full range of nightly entertainment. The Inverurie Day Spa & Salon (see page 176) deserves special mention. A large variety of holistic treatments utilizing organic products are provided by internationally trained staff. "The emphasis is all on you, the client," said Karen Urwin, the spa manager, a recent immigrant from Great Britain. The signature treatment is a couple's massage done in the hotel room or suite followed by a candle-light dinner on the balcony.

$$$$ EP, BP, MAP.

Fairmont Southampton Princess

The Fairmont Southampton Princess is the sister resort of the Fairmont Hamilton Princess. The resort is an expansive luxury complex set atop the highest point on the island and offers stunning panoramic views of the South Shore, ocean and surrounding lush tropical gardens and golf course.

All rooms have views either of the Great Sound, the South Shore or the golf course. Facilities include a secluded private beach club with an adjoining bar and restaurant, indoor heated pool with waterfalls and gardens, tennis courts and pro shop, health club with state-of-the-art Cybex equipment, and a shopping arcade with a beauty salon. All guest rooms are air-conditioned. There is a choice of nine restaurants - six at the Southampton Princess and three at the sister

Resort, the Hamilton Princess, several bars and lounges with nightly entertainment, and an 18-hole golf course. Scuba diving, snorkeling, fishing and other water sports can be arranged.

The 31,000 square foot Willow Stream Spa facility with 15 treatment rooms deserves special mention. Whether you are looking for a simple massage or a pampering rejuvenating treatment from head to toe, you will not be disappointed. Lush with the natural aromatherapy of its tropical surroundings, the spa's atmosphere echoes the elegance of the resort itself and the energy of Bermuda.

$$$$ MAP.

Grotto Bay Beach Hotel & Tennis Club

The views from the guest rooms are spectacular. The pastel shades of the hotel's guest units are flanked by the glistening waters of Castle Harbour and the great causeway that leads across it. The resort's private beach has two secluded coves within an enclosed bay. There's a deep-water dock, freshwater pool with swim-up bar and an outdoor hot tub.

Two 500,000 year-old underground grottos on the property deserve special mention, especially as you are permitted to take a dip amidst the stalactites: a unique aquatic experience to the not so faint-hearted traveler.

There are 201 well-appointed rooms in 11 three-story coral colored lodges, featuring native Bermudian architecture. The majority of buildings are close to the water's edge, but some require a bit of a hike up a hill. Be sure to ask about the location when reserving a room, especially if you have trouble walking. The best rooms are, of course, those on the lower levels, overlooking the

213

sound. Those on the upper levels offer views of the complex and Castle Harbour beyond and are no less inspiring. All have been refurbished and redecorated and are only a little less luxurious than those of the great resort hotels on the South Shore. The ground floor rooms are wheelchair accessible (check availability when booking).

The restaurants – there are three on site – cater to most tastes. Easy, informal dining can be found at the Palm Court which has recently undergone major redecoration and renovation. Stately palms, terra cotta tiles and trade wind motifs deliver a tropical atmosphere for casual dining. The menu is island inspired. The Palm Court also features an elegant bar ready to serve a full range of exotic cocktails. The newly renovated Hibiscus Room offers an elegant dining experience amidst soft hues of coral, beige and crisp white echoing tropical sophistication of Bermuda. The menu, which changes daily, includes fine European cuisine with Bermudian flavor.

The dress code is smart casual. Jacket and tie are optional. The Bayside Bar & Grill is situated by the pool and is only steps from the sea. Quick foods like hamburgers, hot-dogs, sandwiches and salads are on the menu, as are a savory Island BBQ on Monday evenings and a fresh Seafood Soiree on Thursdays (seasonal and weather permitting).

This is a great resort for families with children, especially young ones. If there is a downside to Grotto Bay (and I don't think there is) some might say it is the small beach, and it definitely can become crowded at times. The large pools, patios and lawns, where you can seek all the sunshine you want, more than make up for the lack of sand and surf. I recommend you take advantage of the MAP dining plan. It costs only $58 per person per day and is an excellent value, even with the added 15% gratuity.

The hotel has four all-weather tennis courts, a resident tennis pro, a pro shop, and offers water-skiing, snorkeling and parasailing from its own dock. There is a premium 5 Star PADI Dive facility – Triangle Diving (www.trianglediving.com) – on site, offering certification courses, advanced courses and daily dives from a boat that is stationed at the resort. Golf can be arranged on any of three nearby courses. Scooter rentals and bus stop are right outside the hotel.

$$$, EP, BP, MAP.

Grotto Bay Beach Hotel, 11 Blue Whole Hill, Hamilton

Parish, CR 04, Bermuda, _ 441-293-8333,

Fax 441-293-2306, www.grottobay.com

The Reefs Hotel & Club Bermuda

The Reefs Hotel and Club, one of Bermuda's smaller resorts, sits high on the cliffs overlooking its own private beach on Christian Bay. You have to visit this one-of-a-kind resort to really appreciate it. It has an atmosphere all its own, but it's hard to define exactly where it stems from. Maybe it's the sometimes misty views overlooking the ocean and beach from the terraced rooms and cottages. Maybe it's the people who work there; they certainly seem to be happier than most hotel staff, at the least the ones I've run into over the past years. Maybe it's the South Shore – everything is special on the South Shore.

The facilities at the Reefs Hotel and Club are outstanding, as they should be for a resort of this class and the amount of money that's been spent on it. Much smaller than its glitzier neighbors and competitors, it comprises only 67 units, making for a quieter, more intimate hotel. Small as it is, it boasts three restaurants, catering to tastes as varied as you can imagine. Coconuts deserves a special mention. According to Frommers, "there's no finer or more romantic spot in Bermuda for an alfresco sunset dinner than this beach terrace" and that is absolutely true, unless, of course, one compares it to a romantic dinner served right on the beach beneath the stars, complete with tiki torches and accompanied by the rhythm of the waves. This ultimate in romantic dining experience is also offered at The Reefs, but advance reservations are required.

There's also a fitness center, an infinity pool (the most beautiful one I have ever seen), two all-weather tennis courts, complimentary kayaking (a great feature, considering its location on the South Shore), and you can rent snorkeling equipment; scooters can be rented across the street. Watersports and golf can be arranged by the hotel staff; just give them a little advance notice. The resort comes highly recommended, by me, but it's expensive. Rates start at around $249 for a double off season and go up from there, but they do include a MAP dining plan, and you get exactly what you pay for: a quality vacation to remember.

Verdict: A small, intimate resort more for adult couples than kids. The private beach is small but about as good as it gets. The resort always seems be busy. Three nice restaurants. Friendly staff. A bit too upscale for some, perhaps, but the overall experience is above average.

Practical Information:

$$$$ MAP, BP.

The Reefs, 56 South Road, Southampton, SN 02, Bermuda,

441-238-0222, 800-742-2008 (USA & Canada), fax 441-238-8372, www.thereefs.com

Tucker's Point Hotel and Spa Bermuda

The Tucker's Point Hotel and Spa is an elegant Bermuda luxury hotel located on more than 200 acres of

Bermuda's most exclusive ocean front property in Tucker's Town. Tucker's Point Hotel and Spa opened in April of 2009 and is Bermuda's latest addition to its lineup of luxury hotels and the centerpiece of the Tucker's Point Club, a resort, private club and residential community.

The hotel features 88 guestrooms, including 20 suites - 13 of which have fireplaces - each with large, private balconies or terraces and commanding ocean views. The furnishings are exquisite, the bathrooms spacious, and the in-room amenities are extensive: wireless internet access, a flat screen TV, in-room safe, iPod dock, and five-fixture bath. Superior and deluxe guest rooms measure 500 square foot and 600 square foot respectively, while suites average 1,200 square foot.

Other amenities include a private beach with beautiful pink sand; a day-sailing marina & dive shop, 2 swimming pools, croquet court, fitness center, a 5,000 square foot conference center; a world-class spa with 11 treatment rooms and cabanas, garden sanctuary with Yoga and Tai Chi lawn; complimentary Wi-Fi, business center and IT support.

There are four 4 tennis courts, and an 18-hole golf course

Dining options include The Point Restaurant, Wine Room (private dining), The Library, and 24-hour room service.

The hotel is situated in Tucker's Town, Hamilton Parish, just a short drive from the airport.

Contact:
Tucker's Point Hotel & Spa
60 Tucker's Point Drive
Tucker's Town, HS 02
441 298 4000

Note: I have visited all of the above resorts, stayed in most, and just looked at the others. As far as I can tell, they all provide good clean accommodations and fair value for money. That being said, due to changing times and circumstances, I can make no recommendations, specific or implied, and therefore cannot accept any responsibility for any problems you may experience during your stay at any of the hotels and resorts I have reviewed.

Small Hotels:

Bermuda small hotels are the true face of the island's accommodations. They reflect the intimacy of the smaller facility but they are not short on amenities. Most are large enough to offer dining room service, bars, pools and patios, and some even have their own beach. Many have international reputations and enjoy repeat visitations from their guests. Bermuda Small Hotels include Grape Bay Beach, Pompano, Rosedon, Surfside Beach Club, and The Wharf Executive Suites. The smaller Bermuda hotels are typically family-owned establishments. Most have a restaurant, pool and/or beach. Some have a spa and watersports facilities, and most of them will fit the more modest budget, although you'll find that some are just as expensive, and opulent, as their larger peers - the resorts. Here's a complete listing of Bermuda's Small Hotels:

9 Beaches Resort Bermuda

Guests at 9 Beaches Bermuda can enjoy sophisticated and civilized Bermuda and leave the formal attire at home. At 9 Beaches Resort Bermuda, cabana lodgings are comfortably chic, flip flops are fashionable, and neither jackets nor ties are required. With rates starting at $280 double occupancy, including a full, hot breakfast daily, 9 Beaches gives beach lovers a nature lover's paradise, mouth-watering cuisine and water sports galore at an affordable price.

If you're really looking for an out-of-the-way retreat, 9 Beaches Bermuda is the place for you. If you've ever been to Bermuda before, or think you know the island, it really is time to think again. There was a time when 9 Beaches Resort was a bit "iffy." The 9 Beaches Bermuda has, however, undergone some major renovations and is now more than up to par. I consider it be one of the last great romantic getaways on earth.

"Guests who love 9 Beaches love the ocean, the outdoors and want to just relax and have fun, and know they are getting a good value for the vacation dollars," says General Manager Robin Gilbert. To commemorate its 400th anniversary, Bermuda will celebrate with tall ships, festivals, performances and exhibitions that honor the island's culture and heritage.

Situated on the westernmost tip of Bermuda, 9 Beaches boasts 360 degrees of spectacular seascapes in an eco-friendly setting. Nine separate beaches provide endless options for enjoying and relaxing. Each stylish cabana offers views of the Atlantic. Dining can be arranged anywhere on the resort via the roaming dining service a La Cart. From the programmable cell phone provided upon check-in, service is just a call away. For reservations call 866-841-9009.

Contact:

9 Beaches, Box MA 238, Sandys Bermuda MA BX,
Tel: 1-441-239-2999

Bay City Guest House Bermuda

Bay City Guest House is a small, upscale hotel set in downtown Hamilton; it's an ideal venue for business travelers. Many of the rooms offer inspiring views of the harbor, which is just across the street.

Room 9 with its hot tub and panoramic views is quite special, while room number 12, a corporate suite, has an ornamental fireplace, a large flat-screen TV, and a king-size bed. The guest house a pleasant breakfast room which overlooks the harbor. , is a pleasant place to start the day. There's also a kitchen for those who might like to do it themselves, though I can't for the life of me think why they would - all the amenities of downtown Hamilton are just a step away. Unfortunately, there's no pool, no beach, and the reception staff is present only between 9am and 5pm.

Practical Information:

10 rooms, 2 suites

In-room: safe, Wi-Fi.

In-hotel: bar, Internet terminal, Wi-Fi hotspot.

Rate includes: Continental breakfast

Credit Cards: AE, MC, V

$$

Contact:

Bay City Guest House

53 Pitts Bay Rd., Hamilton, HM 06

Phone: 441/295-1275

www.baycity.bm

Coco Reef Resort

Coco Reef Hotel Bermuda (formerly Stonington Beach Hotel) is really more a resort than simply a hotel. Recently renovated, this small resort is perhaps one of Bermuda's best kept secrets. Coco Reef Bermuda is a beachfront property located on the Island's popular

South Shore, famous for its long stretches of beautiful pink sand and emerald waters. The hotel overlooks the South Shore in Paget Parish and is only steps away from the world famous Elbow Beach. It has 64 comfortable rooms with half of them oceanfront and the rest ocean view, a private beach, a sunken bar, library, freshwater pool and a sundeck.

Elements of Bermuda's history are found throughout the property, a fountain here, an exotic statue there, antique furniture accents throughout as well as some period paintings reflecting the days of Spanish colonial rule. Even the elegant, first-rate restaurant Juanito's is named after Bermuda's discoverer, Juan de Bermudez. The menu is eclectic and there is a large selection of European and American wines.

All 64 guestrooms have been refurbished, feature wicker furniture, and have been tastefully decorated in the traditional pastel colors of Bermuda. Each guest room features either a balcony or patio, air conditioning, cable TV, direct dial telephones, hairdryer, iron and ironing board, coffee maker, in-room safe, mini-refrigerator, and private bathroom amenities.

Coco Reef boasts a swimming pool, two tennis courses, two restaurants, concierge service, a library, free internet access and business services.

The hotel is conveniently located on the South Road with easy access by bus to the city of Hamilton and the Royal Naval Dockyard. Nearby attractions include the Bermuda Botanical Gardens, Elbow Beach, and the Railway Trail.

Hamilton is just 10 minutes away by bus or taxi. There are two all-weather tennis courts, a golf course nearby; snorkeling from the hotel's beach and other sports can be arranged.

Verdict: Great place to stay, nice rooms, friendly and attentive staff.

$$$$ MAP, BP.

Coco Reef Bermuda, 3 Stonington Circle, South Shore Road, Paget Parish, PG 04, Bermuda, 441-236-5416, fax 441-236-9766

Grape Bay Beach Hotel Bermuda

Grape Bay Beach Hotel (formerly White Sands & Cottages) is a secluded Bermuda retreat, extensively renovated and given new life as the Grape Bay Beach Hotel.

Two classes of rooms are available: the Garden View rooms have balconies and offer a choice of either king beds or 2 doubles. The Superior Rooms offer spectacular ocean views of the Atlantic; most have king sized beds.

The main lobby and all rooms have received a nice facelift; the poolside snack bar was converted to a first class restaurant, Sapori that serves three meals daily. While the hotel is set in landscaped gardens, the Grape Bay Beach is a short stroll away. There is a large freshwater pool and a sun terrace, all within easy reach of Hamilton and nearby golf courses.

The hotel is on the South Road bus route to both Hamilton and the Royal Naval Dockyard. It's a bit of a walk to the bus stop but the hotel does offer shuttle service to it.

Verdict: a budget hotel and you get exactly what you pay for. The rooms are spacious and clean and you'll enjoy wonderful ocean view. It's very quiet and relaxing. Not quite up to the standard of the more pricy of Bermuda's offering, but fair value for money.

$$ MAP, BP, EP.

Grape Bay Beach Hotel, PO Box 174, Paget PG BX, Bermuda, 441-236-2023, fax 441-236-2486

Hamiltonian Hotel and Island Club Bermuda

The Hamiltonian Hotel and Island Club is located atop Langton Hill, affording a spectacular view of Pembroke Parish, the City of Hamilton, the North Shore and the whole chain of Bermuda Islands.

The resort offers 32 ocean-view one-bedroom suites in tropical garden settings, all equipped with refrigerator, microwave, toaster and coffee maker. The resort's pool, overlooks the Atlantic Ocean. If you love tennis, you can play a set of two on the resort's three tennis courts (two are lighted for evening play) and you can play golf at any of Bermuda's nine golf courses. Along Bermuda's beach areas, you can enjoy sailing, snorkeling, and scuba diving. Golf and bicycling are among the most popular sports. Just a mile from the resort, you'll find yourself on world-famous Front Street, a shopper's paradise.

Verdict: While we've heard some great things about this small resort ("The room was clean, the views were breathtaking, and the staff was accommodating and addressed all of our concerns quickly. We would definitely stay there again."), we've also heard a few negative comments (An average place. Needs renovating. Few TV channels. Window A/C units etc.). So what to think... Well, as always, you get what you pay for, and this is not a high-end resort. The big advantages as I see them are the location, the seclusion, the views and, yes, the chance to experience Bermuda from an entirely different perspective. Not the best choice of hotel in Bermuda, but certainly not the worst.

$$$ MAP, BP.

Hamiltonian Hotel & Island Club, PO Box HM 1738, Hamilton, HM GX, Bermuda, 441-295- 5608, fax 441-295-7481.

Pompano Beach Club Bermuda

Pompano Beach Club is a family-owned Bermuda hotel that started out, as its name implies, as a private fishing club. After a day of deep-sea fishing, club members would and cook their catch. A restaurant was added to the club and that was soon followed by a hotel. Today, Pompano Beach Club is a popular 74-room beach resort.

The Pompano Beach Club has its own private beach on a shallow sandbar. At low tide, its possible wade out almost 300 yards in warm waters that never each above chest height. The resort facilities include a heated pool, a children's pool and 3 outdoor Jacuzzis.

Guests can avail themselves of complimentary fishing tackle and bait and fish from the hotel's private dock. There's also a watersports center on the beach where you can rent a variety of equipment including windsurfing boards, sailboats and ocean kayaks. Snorkel equipment and sea scooters can be rented and the nearby reefs offer endless opportunities to explore the resort's underwater world.

The hotel offers a fitness center, table tennis, air hockey and table football in the games room, and an outdoor tennis court with complimentary rackets and balls.

The hotel is adjacent to the world-famous Port Royal Golf Course and guests can book tee times when making their hotel reservation. They also offer year-round golf packages and will gladly ferry your clubs to and from the course free of charge.

All of the guest rooms Pompano Beach Club have private bathrooms, air conditioning, a small refrigerator, hair dryer, iron, ironing board, telephone, clock radio, safe and cable TV.

Meals are served in the evening in the hotel's Cedar Room, and there's a dress code: smart casual – men are not required to wear jackets but shirts with collars are a must - jeans, shorts and t-shirts are not allowed. The menu changes daily but you can also go off-site to dine at other nearby hotels, including Cambridge Beaches and The Reefs.

The resort cocktail bar offers evening entertainment throughout the summer months and the Pool Bar is open daily and serves lunch including gourmet salads, deli-sandwiches and nachos.

Scooter are available for rent at the hotel. A shuttle service is offered to the nearby bus stop for guests who like to use public transport - the bus stop is at the hotel's entrance. From here, you can easily reach Royal Naval Dockyard and Hamilton. The hotel also provides complimentary transport to the ferry stop at Rockaway where guests can take the aquatic route to Hamilton.

Verdict: One of Bermuda's best kept secrets. It's been said that the beach seemed a little on the small side, but we can tell you that it's rarely overcrowded. The ocean is crystal clear and great for wading, swimming and snorkeling; great for the kids. Real value for the money.

$$ MAP, BP, EP

Pompano Beach Club, 36 Pompano Beach Road, SB 03, Bermuda - 800-343-4155

Newstead Belmont Hills Golf Resort and Spa

Newstead Belmont Hills Golf Resort and Spa is perhaps the best thing that has happened to Bermuda in a couple of decades. I stayed at the resort some four years ago, just before it closed for extensive renovations and revamping, and it was a great place to stay then, even though it was a little dated. Located in Paget Parish, just across the Great Sound from Hamilton, I have fond memories of the Newstead resort.

Perhaps the most vivid of those memories, aside from its extraordinarily comfortable cottages set on a hillside overlooking the Great Sound, is the view across the Sound of Hamilton by night - breathtaking. Today, after all the work has been done, Newstead Golf Resort and Spa has taken its rightful place among the leading resort and golf destinations on the island. Yes, the resort is up for sale, but it remains open and just as inviting as ever.

The Newstead Belmont Hills Resort features 45 one, two- and three-bedroom suites and studios, each with a private balcony featuring views from the garden to the infinity pool to Hamilton Harbour. You'll also enjoy a full-function kitchen, luxurious bathroom and an inviting living area where you'll discover a fresh take on Bermuda's old-world charm – and with all the comfort and convenience of home.

Amenities at the resort include a semi-private, 18-hole golf course, a first-rate spa, two fine restaurants, a fitness room, business center, two tennis courts, and infinity pool, whirlpool, and its own ferry dock to provide easy transportation to the City of Hamilton and the Royal Naval Dockyard. Unfortunately, there's no beach on the property, but the South Shore and all it has to offer is less than 10 minutes away by bus.

The Spa at Newstead Belmont Hills is located at the east end of the resort. Large windows take full advantage of the sweeping view of Hamilton Harbour. A "wet room" and multiple treatment rooms affords guests perfect privacy.

Verdict: Newstead has always been one of my favorite hotels in Bermuda. So, whether you're visiting Bermuda to relax or seeking adventure, if you make your base camp at Newstead, there are a multitude of activities and experiences available. And I have no problem recommending it to you.

$$$ MAP, BP.

Newstead Belmont Hills Golf Resort & Spa, 27 Harbour Rd, Paget, Bermuda PG02 441-236-0608

Rosedon Bermuda

Rosedon is a small resort hotel on the outskirts of Hamilton in Pembroke County. The main house has Colonial rooms in modern wings and wide verandahs overlooking magnificent gardens. All the guest rooms are air-conditioned, have coffee makers, refrigerators, radio, TV, telephones and safety deposit boxes.

I stayed at Rosedon a couple of years ago. It reminds me of one of the great antebellum mansions of America's Old South. A great white house with a columned front porch that stretches the entire width of the house, where a traditional English breakfast is served with pride and flair. The gardens are spectacular, awash with the colors of giant hibiscus blooms, birds of paradise, and banana plants.

There are two large, antique-filled lounges, with TVs and self-service bars – the honor system prevails – and there's a heated freshwater pool and sun deck. Unfortunately, there isn't a restaurant on the property – there are several nearby and just down the road in

Hamilton – but breakfast is included in the rate. Afternoon tea is a tradition at Rosedon and worth hurrying back for. Hamilton is a 10- minute walk away (five minutes by bus or the hotel's free shuttle service) and tennis is available by arrangement with South Shore Beach and Tennis Club or at Stonington Beach, both served by the hotel's free shuttle service.

Verdict: Not really a hotel for families with small children, but ideal for older couples and business travelers. It's a bit on the expensive side, but not prohibitively so.

$$$ BP, EP.

Rosedon, PO Box 290, Hamilton, HM AX, Bermuda, 441- 295-1640, 800-742-5008, fax 441-295-5904

Waterloo House Bermuda

A small hotel on the harbor with a secluded courtyard and gardens and a wonderful view of the Great Sound, Waterloo House Bermuda, is only a three-minute walk from downtown Hamilton, has an elegant dining room, a bar, a library, a small freshwater pool and a sun deck. Rooms are all air-conditioned and meals are served either in the dining room or on the Harbour Front Terrace. Once a private home, the old house has been enlarged and extensively remodeled.

The addition of five cottages, bringing the total number of guest units up to 30, and its close proximity to Hamilton, has turned it into the ideal business hotel. But it's a great vacation destination, if you are not bothered about its lack of beach. The guest rooms are furnished mainly with English antiques that impart a somewhat old-world atmosphere.

There are terraced gardens that descend to the harbor wall, and there's a lawn with tables and beach umbrellas where you can sit, take it easy, and enjoy the view and a drink before dinner. The main dining room is adjacent to the lawn and also offers views across the Great Sound.

Warm and charming; could become a habit. Many people book again and again.

Verdict: Again, we've heard good things and bad things about this once top-of-line hotel. The consensus seems to be that it's a bit run-down, whatever that might mean. Our experience is that the hotel is a really charming place, but is currently a bit overpriced.

$$$ MAP, BP.

Waterloo House, PO Box HM, 333, Hamilton, HM BX, Bermuda, 441-295-4480, 800-468-4100, fax 441-295-2585

Royal Palms Hotel Bermuda

The Royal Palms Hotel is a turn-of-the century private home converted into a small exclusive hotel in a quiet residential area a short walk from downtown Hamilton. There are 12 comfortable guest rooms, lovely landscaped gardens, and an elegant restaurant and cocktail lounge. Outdoor dining is available during the summer months.

Verict: This is one hotel I have no personal experience of, except for a quick looksee visit. Doing a little re4seach it seems that no one has anything bad to say about the place, quite the reverse in fact. One lady had this to say: "I can't say enough about how lovely everything was. We were treated like royalty and hated to leave. The front desk staff was superb, even driving us to town one evening." That, I think, is quite a recommendation.

$$ CP.

The Royal Palms Hotel, PO Box HM 499, Hamilton, HM CX, Bermuda, 441-292-1854, 800-678-0785, fax 441-292- 1946

The St. George's Club

The St. George's Club, on Rose Hill in St. George's, is a full-service cottage colony with 18 acres of landscaped gardens, a three-floor clubhouse, a gourmet restaurant, lounge, English-style pub and a convenience store. All of the cottages overlook either the harbor or the Robert Trent Jones golf course. They are all fully equipped with a kitchen, living room and dining room, have TVs and are air-conditioned.

The resort has three freshwater swimming pools, three all-weather tennis courts, a beach club, and the golf course. The staff will arrange a variety of watersports from charter fishing to scuba diving. At Blackbeard's Hideout, enjoy outdoor dining for lunch or dinner at the local favorite restaurant, overlooking Achilles Bay and Ft. St. Catherine. No visit to Bermuda is complete without experiencing the excitement of Blackbeard's at least once.

$$$$ EP. The St. George's Club, PO Box GE 92, St. George's GE BX,

Surf Side Beach Club Bermuda

Surf Side Beach Club is a unique hideaway and peaceful haven overlooking the ocean with all the services of a larger hotel including restaurant and bar, beauty salon and mini-spa. The delightful cottages - apartments and suites are nestled into the natural cliffside terraces and gardens leading to the private beach. Surf Side is advantageously located within easy reach of Hamilton for shopping and business - for touring and for sports pursuits like golf, tennis, sailing, scuba and deep sea fishing.

The hotel restaurant, The Palms Restaurant and Bar is open daily for breakfast - lunch and dinner and we can vouch for the quality of the food that was served when we were there. Reservations advised.

Verdict: I stayed at Surf Side, with my family, a little more than three years ago so I know what I'm talking about. The four days we were there we were treated so well that the hotel is always forefront in my memory when I think of my next trip to the island. The rooms were impressive, the views spectacular, and the beach, though very small and located at the bottom of long flight of stone steps, is gorgeous. Everything is within easy reach: all the great beaches on the South Shore are just a short bus ride away via bus route 7, as is the city of Hamilton.

$$$ EP, BP, MAP.

Surf Side Beach Club, South Rd, Warwick Parish, Bermuda 441-236- 7100, 800-553-9990 (Canada& USA), fax, 441-236- 9765

Note: I have visited all of the above small hotels and resorts, stayed in some, and just looked at the others. As far as I can tell, they all provide good clean accommodations and fair value for money. That being said, due to changing times and circumstances, I can make no recommendations, specific or implied, and therefore cannot accept any responsibility for any problems you may experience during your stay at any of the hotels and resorts I have reviewed.

Guest Houses:

One of the best "where to stay" options on the island is Bermuda's Guest Houses. More Bed and Breakfast inns than hotels, these often quaint little homes-come-hotels offer plenty of personal service, good food, and owners who care about you and want to make your stay a memorable one. Rates range from budget to expensive, but you always get at least a little more than you pay for. Bermuda Guest Houses are not quite the well-kept secret they once were, but pick the right time of your to go and you can bet you have plenty of peace, quiet and a rare view of Bermuda living as few get to see it. Here are some options:

Aunt Nea's Inn at Hillcrest

Aunt Nea's Inn at Hillcrest is an old house in the Colonial style, built sometime around 1750. It sits on a hill overlooking the Harbour. A very pleasant place to stay, this is one of Bermuda's best-kept secrets, though the word is getting around and things can sometimes get quite busy.

Aunt Nea's Inn at Hillcrest offers 14 guest rooms; most of them have bathrooms with showers and five have Jacuzzis. The guest rooms all feature four- poster beds, some of unusual design. All rooms are air-conditioned; none have TVs, although there is one in the sitting room. Continental breakfast is included in the rate, and tea or coffee is available throughout the day at no charge. The Town of St. George is just a short distance away and the local beaches are also within easy reach, either on foot or by bus.

$$ Aunt Nea's Inn at Hillcrest, 1 Nea's Alley, Old Maid's Lane, St.

George GE BX, Bermuda. 441-297-1630, fax 441-297-1908, www.auntneas.com.

Astwood Cove Guest Apartments - Bermuda

Astwood Cove Guest Apartments in Warwick Paris, are owned by Cameron and Deirdre Hill. Located close to the South Shore at its beautiful beaches, Astwood Cove features lush, landscaped sub-tropical gardens and one of the nicest private swimming pools in Bermuda. Each self-contained Studio and Suite is air-conditioned with its own private patio and fully equipped kitchenette. The complex is right on the bus route just 4 miles from Hamilton in a peaceful spot overlooking Bermuda's South Shore and is within easy reach of the island's golf courses, tennis clubs, scuba diving outfitters, snorkeling spots, and horseback riding. Maid service is provided daily.

Room Information:

Standard Studio

Ideal for one or two people some studios can accommodate a third on the pull out sofa - daily maid service - room has two twin beds and can be made up as a king bed - Max occupancy 3.

Superior Studio

This apartment offers views of parkland and ocean - Ideal for one or two people - some studios can accommodate a third on the pull out sofa - daily maid service - room has two twin beds and can be made up as a king bed - has private balcony - Max occupancy 3.

Standard Suite

These one bedroom self-catering apartments can sleep 2 additional guests on the sofa-bed - Some can sleep a third additional guest in the bedroom - Full kitchenette - Private patio - daily maid service - contains two twin beds that can be made up as a king bed - Max occupancy 5.

Superior Suite

One bedroom self-catering apartments can sleep 2 additional guests on the sofa bed in living room - Offers views of parkland and ocean - contains two twin beds that can be made up as a king bed - Full kitchenette - daily maid service. Max occupancy 4.

$$$ From $150 per night

Contact: Astwood Cove Guest Apartments, 49 South Road, Warwick, Bermuda: 800/637-4116 in the U.S, 441/236-0984

The Corals, Bermuda - Bed and Breakfast

The Corals, Bermuda, is one of those neat little B&B accommodations you find in odd little places all around the world; almost always they are operated by owners of English extraction. This one is set in the quaint little parish of Somerset, not far from the Royal Naval Dockyard and within easy reach of the buses and ferries. The Corals is an "old Bermuda" farmhouse, fully restored and still a much-loved family home, but with a difference. The owners, Paul and Judith Chambers are offering Bed and Breakfast for two, and they plan to add room for more lately in 2012.

Ok, so you're looking for something a little special, a little different, maybe a quiet romantic visit, maybe even your honeymoon, or perhaps you just want to relax and get away from it all. If so, then this is probably a very good choice for you, because no matter how long you would like to stay, these two good folks would love to "put you up," and they will make sure you are well looked after. Paul and Judith are both big on customer service; they will even help you with planning activities, both before and during your stay. Just let them know what you need.

Services Include:

A separate entrance from main house; you'll have full use of the furnished and fully equipped courtyard, including the BBQ; You'll have your own, en-suite bathroom; reverse-cycle air conditioning; there's also an indoor dining area; and you'll have Cable TV, free Wi-Fi, Hi-fi with cd, radio and iPod dock; Airport transfers can be arranged; and they'll help you plan and book your activities.

If you'd like to know more, or would like to book a stay, you can either visit the Corals website, or you can send an email to bookings@thecoralsbermuda.com.

Edgehill Manor Bermuda

Edgehill Manor is an old Bermuda home in a quiet residential area within easy walking distance of Hamilton's shops and the harbor. Most of the spacious rooms have private balconies. Semi-tropical gardens and a freshwater swimming pool.

Owner, Bridget M Marshall, is a great cook and she invites you to feast on her home-baked continental breakfast featuring various muffins, her famous Pear and Walnut Coffee Cake, Apple Cake, Sour Cream Coffee Cake and much more.

All nine rooms at Edgehill are decorated in the style of an English country residence and come with en suite bathroom, private balcony or terrace, air conditioning, a small refrigerator, microwave oven, cable TV, safe, clock radio and private telephone line (local calls free). Guests can relax in the sub-tropical garden or around the freshwater pool. Edgehill Manor doesn't serve dinner, which is not really surprising considering the large number of excellent restaurants nearby.

Note: at the time of writing, this establishment did not accept credit cards.

$ CP. Edgehill Manor, PO Box HM1048, Hamilton, HM EX, Bermuda, 441-295-7124, fax 441-295-3850.

Erith Guest House Bermuda

Erith Guest House Bermuda - gotta be the nicest of them all - is located on a quiet back road in Paget Parish. It's an old Bermuda Home recently renovated and upgraded. Now one of Bermuda's newest guest houses, the property features seven guest rooms, a one bedroom suite, swimming pool and Jacuzzi hot tub. Erith Guest House is owned by Kieran Campbell and opened in June of 2003.

The accommodations comprise six standard rooms, a superior room and a one-bedroom suite. All rooms are fully air conditioned and offer cable TV, telephone, internet connection, iron, hairdryer, safe, microwave oven, fridge and kettle. The superior room has a kitchenette and private patio; the suite has a full kitchen and private balcony. All ground floor rooms have private entrances.

Paget Parish is a quiet section of Bermuda across the Great Sound from Hamilton – just a short ferry ride. There are plenty of activities available – hiking, biking, the beaches on the South Shore - or you can simply relax by the pool, sip a cocktail and read a book. Erith Guest House is close to the city of Hamilton (Bermuda's

Capital) and its shops; the Bermuda Botanical Gardens and Paget Marsh just a short distance away from the guest house and Belmont Hills Golf Course is less than five minutes away. If you're intending to rent a bicycle or moped, Oleander Cycles is just down the road.

Contact: Erith Guest House, 15 Pomander Road, Paget PG 05, Bermuda; Tel: (441) 232-827 or (441) 535-6369

Note: I have visited all of the above guest houses and hotels, stayed in some, and just looked at the others. As far as I can tell, they all provide good clean accommodations and fair value for money. That being said, due to changing times and circumstances, I can make no recommendations, specific or implied, and therefore cannot accept any responsibility for any problems you may experience during your stay at any of the hotels and resorts I have reviewed.

Public Transport Information
The Buses and Bus Schedules:

Bermuda has one of the easiest to use public bus services in the world. The system is divided in 14 fare zones of about 2 miles length and fares are based on the number of zones travelled. Buses require exact fare in local currency, tokens, or prepaid tickets; transfers are available. Single- or multiple-day transportation passes, accepted on buses and ferries, can be purchased. Children under age five ride free, and at age 5–15 pay a reduced rate.

Bus Schedules: If you have the correct time – watch, cell phone, whatever – you don't need to worry too much about the actual schedules - I never have - because no matter where you might be on the island, or at what time, so long as it's between 7 am and 11 pm, there's always a bus just around the corner, just a few minutes away. They run at variable (often 15-minute) intervals; so, as they say, there'll be another one along in just a minute. All you need do is find one of those pink (inbound towards Hamilton) or Blue (outbound from Hamilton) poles they are everywhere - then stand and wait. Buses stop at them on request. – You won't wait for long, I promise.

There are pink and blue bus stop poles on the roads at all of the major hotels, guest houses, resorts and cottage colonies

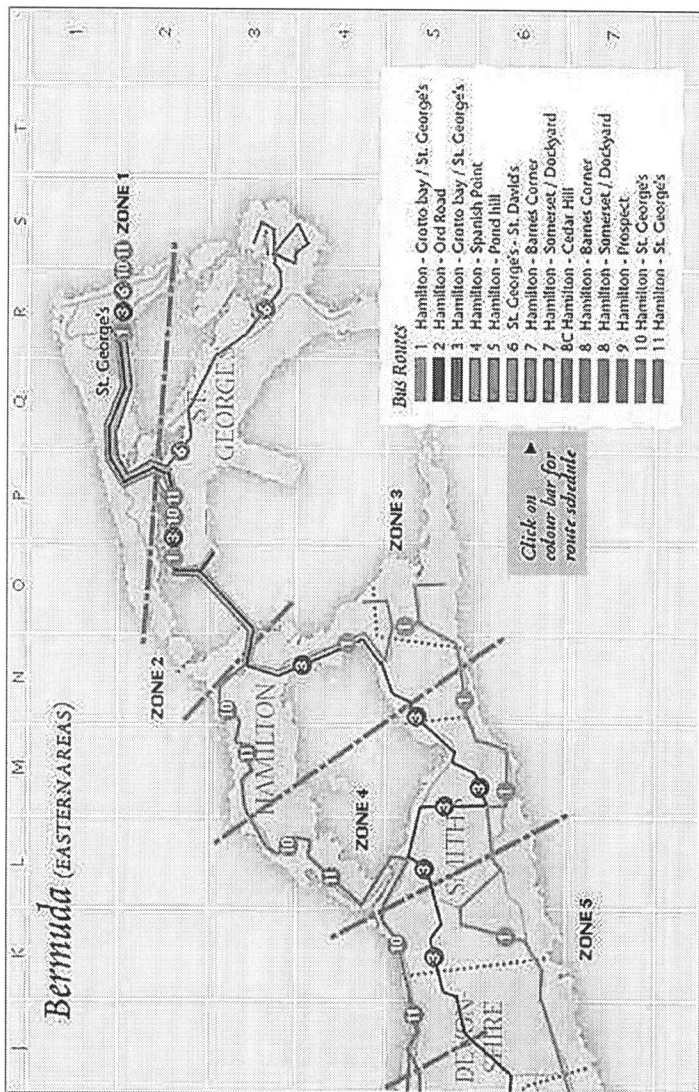

The East Bus System Map

238

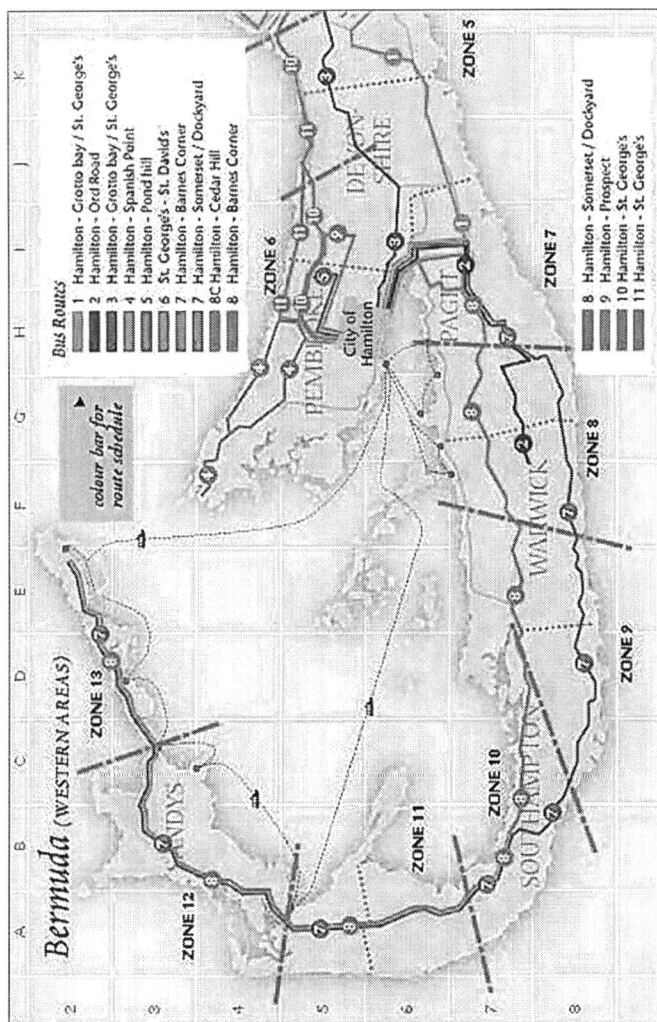

The West Bus System Map

Most visitors from cruise ships use the bus system; however, airline passengers cannot transport luggage on the buses and generally prefer the taxi or airport limo system.

All but one route start from the bus terminal in Hamilton.

Route 1 – Round trip from Hamilton to Grotto Bay and St. George's

Route 2 - Round trip from Hamilton to Ord Road

Route 3 - Round trip from Hamilton to Grotto Bay and St. George's

Route 4 - Round trip from Hamilton to Spanish Point

Route 5 - Round trip from Hamilton to Pond Hill

Route 6 - Round trip from St. George's to St. David's (it's the only way to get there, other than by taxi)

Route 7 - Round trip from Hamilton to Barnes Corner via the beaches on the South Shore Road (this really puts the beaches within easy reach, and quickly.

Route 8 & 8C - Round trip from Hamilton to Barnes Corner; Hamilton to the Dockyard; Hamilton to Somerset via Middle Road

Route 9 - Round trip from Hamilton to Prospect (National Stadium)

Route 10 - Round trip from Hamilton to St. George's via North Shore past Aquarium

Route 11 - Round trip from Hamilton to St. George's via North Shore Road

The Eastern Bus Routes

The Western Bus Routes

Bermuda Ferry Information

On Saturdays the first ferry leaves Hamilton at 8:15 am and the last at 9:45 pm. Sundays & holidays, the first ferry leaves at 10:10, the last at 7 pm. Note that bikes are not allowed on the Pink Route.

Blue Route – Monday to Friday (Hamilton - West End - Dockyard)

Blue Route – Saturday (Hamilton - West End - Dockyard)

Pink Route (Hamilton - Paget - Warwick)
Orange Route (Hamilton - Dockyard - St. George's)
Green Route – Monday to Friday (Hamilton – Rockaway Express)

Thank You:

I sincerely hope you enjoyed this guide book about Bermuda. Thank you so much for purchasing it.

If you have comments of questions, you can contact me by email. At blair@blairhoward.com I will reply to all emails.

And you can also visit my website at www.blairhoward.com to view my blog, and for a complete list of my books.

If you enjoyed the book, I would really appreciate it if you could take a few moments and share your thoughts by posting a review on Amazon. Here's the link to post your review: http://amzn.to/16C4zRG

Other Books by this Author:
Photography Books:

How to Take Better Photographs: Quick and Simple Tips for Improving Your Photographs

Stock Photography: How to take Great Photographs and Sell them Online to Stock Photo Agencies

The Photo Essay: The How to Make Money with your Camera Guide for Writers and Photographers:

Digital Photography - Understanding Composition

Photographer's Guide to Focus and the Sharper Image

Visitor's Guides:

The Visitor's Guide to Florida – A Complete Guide to the Sunshine State

The Visitor's Guide to the Bahamas – The Collection (All three books in one)

The Visitor's Guide to the Bahamas – Grand Bahama Island and Freeport

The Visitor's Guide to the Bahamas – The Out Islands: The Abacos, The Exumas, Eleuthera, The Acklins and More

The Visitor's Guide to the Bahamas – Nassau

Civil War Books

Great Battles of the American Civil War - Chickamauga

Touring Southern Civil War Battlefields: From Vicksburg to Savannah

Battlefields of the Civil War – Visitor's Guide

Made in the USA
Lexington, KY
25 February 2014